Dark Peak

Dalesman Publishing Company
Stable Courtyard, Broughton Hall,
Skipton, North Yorkshire BD23 3AE

First Edition 1997

Text © John Gillham 1997
Cover: Towards Kinder and Bleaklow from
Stanage by Chris Craggs
Maps by Jeremy Ashcroft
Printed by Amadeus Press, Huddersfield

A British Library Cataloguing in Publication
record is available for this book

ISBN 185568 100 5

Dark Peak

John Gillham

Series editor Terry Marsh

DALESMAN

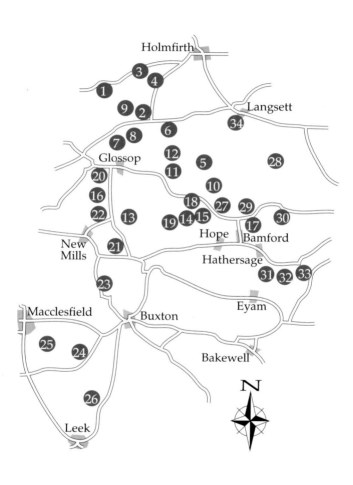

Contents

Publisher's Note

The information given in this book has been provided in good faith and is intended only as a general guide. Whilst all reasonable efforts have been made to ensure that details were correct at the time of publication, the author and Dalesman Publishing Company Ltd cannot accept any responsibility for inaccuracies. It is the responsibility of individuals undertaking outdoor activities to approach the activity with caution and, especially if inexperienced, to do so under appropriate supervision. They should also carry the appropriate equipment and maps, be properly clothed and have adequate footwear. The sport described in this book is strenuous and individuals should ensure that they are suitably fit before embarking upon it.

Introduction

Designated England's first national park, the Peak is also its most popular, serving as a playground to the urban areas of the North and Midlands.

It has two distinct landscapes – the Dark Peak and the White Peak. The Dark Peak, which this book describes, is a stark, simple landscape where dusky millstone grit surfaces from vast peat moors. The latter gets its name from the pale limestone rock that predominates in its intricate valleys and rolling hills, and is described in a companion volume.

While the main body of the Dark Peak lies between Marsden and the Hope valley, two fingers of gritstone extend further south – the eastern edges of Stanage, Curbar and Baslow and the western outliers from Windgather Rocks to Hen Cloud. Ordnance Survey confuse matters by placing these outlying hills in their Outdoor Leisure Map of the White Peak.

Like many walkers I was introduced to the Peak while walking the Pennine Way. Having read the foreboding words of Wainwright about horrid bogs on Bleaklow and Black Hill, I passed these wild places with a certain amount of relief, but looking back on the experience, I enjoyed the rocks of Kinder Scout, and there was a certain amount of masochistic fun in wading through the dark porridge of Black Hill. I was to return many times in subsequent years to find that the Peak had much more to offer with fine walks to remote corners.

Generally, the terrain was a little gentler on the feet than I had remembered. I discovered the true Bleaklow: not the slimy morasses of Bleaklow Head, but places like the rocky Higher Shelf Stones, which can be reached from Glossop using the ancient Doctor's Gate path, and Grinah Stones, a remote jewel approached from the upper Derwent valley.

Nowadays, many of the marshiest areas are straddled by engineered paths of gritstone pavements, brought by helicopter from disused mills to the hilltops. The helicopters still arrive and many of the paths that I describe as grassy or peaty may be paved by the time the walker gets to the hill.

Much has been made of the Dark Peak's eroding vegetation but, away from the popular places such as Kinder, Bleaklow and Black Hill, most of the moorland is cloaked with luxuriant beds of heather, bilberry and cotton grass. Even on the darkest of hills, the little white flowers and bright green leaves of the cloudberry often squeeze through the tangled grasses.

The whole region is a wonderland for walkers who can put up with a little squelch under their feet and a little peat on their socks. They can follow roads used by Roman legions and packhorse trains: they can conjure up sculptures of witches, toadstools, boxing gloves and anvils among the rocks, look across misty horizons to the towns and cities from whence they came, and mingle with climbers by the cliffs and buttresses of Stanage, The Roaches and Froggatt Edge.

Today we all have the freedom to enjoy much of the Peak's uplands, but it has not always been so. In 1932, after many years of abuse from the gamekeepers of the northern grouse moors, the ramblers of Sheffield and Manchester decided to hold a mass trespass. Kinder Scout was the largest section of prohibited land without a footpath and it became their chosen target. A young Manchester rambler, Benny Rothman, headed the publicity and the Manchester Chronicle revealed he would lead the assault on Kinder Scout on Sunday 24 April.

The police, who were anxious to foil the plot, expected Benny to arrive by train and posted officers at Manchester London Road and Hayfield stations. Benny, however, arrived at Hayfield by bicycle to be greeted by hundreds of cheering ramblers. Together they made their way to the old quarry at Bowden Bridge where a brief address was made before continuing towards Kinder Scout. The police were in hot pursuit.

The ramblers made for Kinder's rocky edge only to be greeted and threatened by a score of game-keepers. Exactly how far the ramblers got depends on who you believe, but they did manage to get far enough to join the trespassers from Sheffield who had come up from the Snake Pass. On their return to Hayfield, Benny Rothman was arrested along with five others. At the Derby Assizes, he was given a 4-month gaol sentence for unlawful assembly and breach of the peace.

The trespasses continued, although on a smaller scale, and served to remind the authorities that this was a subject dear to many of the population. It probably led to the formation of the national parks in 1947. The Peak National Park negotiated access with the jealous landowners, and today many thousands roam freely across the wilderness of Kinder and Bleaklow. The ramblers' cause was put into song by folk singer Ewan McColl in *The Manchester Rambler*.

In the book I have described 34 walks ranging from easy summer's evening strolls to a challenging two-day walk across the highest tops. All should be within the scope of a reasonably fit hill walker with some time to spare.

Equipment and safety

It is extremely important that all walkers are fully equipped and practised in the use of map and compass. Their well-being may depend on it one day. The vast moorland spread of the Dark Peak makes it particularly confusing when the mist comes down. It is essential to know exactly where one is and the direction required to get safely off the mountain.

Make sure to take enough food and water – keep additional emergency rations in the corner of the rucksack. Not taking enough food is the quickest way of becoming tired, and being tired is the quickest way of sustaining an injury. Good waterproofs are essential. Remember, getting cold and wet will render the walker vulnerable to hypothermia, even outside the winter months. Modern breathable fabrics, such as those made with Gore-Tex, Cyclone and Sympatex linings, are generally regarded as the best. Some walkers, however, prefer to go for the non-breathable types, which are cheaper, lighter and more compact. Unfortunately, the condensation that forms on the inside of the garments makes the wearer feel wet and uncomfortable when they are taken off.

It is important to wear good walking boots on the hills, for shoes have insufficient grip and ankle support on difficult terrain. Even the lower-level walks can become slippery after rainfall. Many an ankle has been twisted or leg broken for the lack of proper footwear. When snow and ice cover the hills it is more prudent to be equipped with, and know how to use, crampons and an ice-axe. Keep the latter out, once on the slopes, for an ice-axe strapped to a rucksack never saved anyone. It is a good idea to pack some emergency medical supplies (plasters, bandages etc.): there are plenty of good kits available.

Maps

While Jeremy Ashcroft's maps accompanying each walk are beautifully crafted, they are not detailed enough for use in the field. Outdoor Leisure 1:25000 maps are best as they show greater detail including the important field boundaries. The double-sided Ordnance Survey Outdoor Leisure Map of the Dark Peak covers most of the walks in the book, but a few walks on the western gritstone peaks are covered by their White Peak map.

The attractive Harvey's Superwalker maps, Dark

Peak North and Dark Peak South, also cover most of the walks but miss Black Hill and some of the outlying peaks. Harvey's maps are particularly good on upland terrain: they not only show streams but add peat groughs. The walker can plan a walk knowing whether or not it goes through cultivated or semi-cultivated land. Unfortunately, the maps are not so easy to use when it comes to crossing farmland because the field boundaries are missing. This may be offset by their being water-proof and the fact that Peak District paths are usually well waymarked through farmland.

Access

Being part of the Peak National Park, the Dark Peak has many miles of well-preserved footpaths and large areas of agreed access. The boundaries of the access areas are marked on the OS Outdoor Leisure maps with a purple line, and on Harvey's Superwalker maps with a green dotted line. Entry and exit points are marked with an arrow. Walkers should remember however that many of the heather moors are managed for grouse shooting and on shooting days, which will occur between August 12 and December 10, and times of high fire risk, the access areas will be closed to the public with the exception of the rights of way.

Caring for the countryside

With modern methods and increased productivity for the large units, it is becoming much harder for farmers to make a living from the land. Walkers can help by showing consideration for the rural environment, which means shutting gates behind them (except for those that are wedged open), not leaving litter, and by keeping dogs on a lead in sheep country.

Unfortunately, the explosion of people taking to the hills has meant that the footpaths have become eroded. Tom Stephenson's long green trail (the Pennine Way) has been so deeply grooved into the hillsides that various authorities have deemed it necessary to inlay the route with heavy gritstone slabs. There is not a lot the walker can do (except the unthinkable, staying at home) but they can help in a small way:

Avoid walking in very large groups.
Do not walk along the very edge of the footpath, which makes it wider.
If a cart track has one of those pleasant grass islands through the middle, keep it that way by sticking to the stony bits.
Do not wear heavyweight mountain boots for low-level or moorland paths. Use a lightweight pair if possible.
Walk single file across farming land.
You may have a favourite path, but try not to love it to death. Vary your walks and walking areas.

Black Hill and the Saddleworth Edges

Nowhere are the hills of the Dark Peak any darker than Black Hill. The thin soils and the poor drainage make this the most hostile of terrains. Yet Black Hill is a much-maligned hill. A peat fire robbed it of what little vegetation it had and gained for it the same presence as a bowl of cold porridge on a frosty morning. Pennine Wayfarers tackled it with the scathing words of Alfred Wainwright ringing in their ears; their hearts were lighter as they left its bogs behind.

But Black Hill has merits: the ugly can be beautiful. It has the fine gritstone cliffs of Laddow Rocks, the attractive valley of Crowden Brook and wide views from the edges of its plateau. If tackled in summer the peat changes from black morass to a dusky red springboard; easy to walk on, and easy on the feet and knees.

Black Hill's vast western moors decline to the very fringes of the Peak District, where the Saddleworth Edges cap dramatic boulder-strewn slopes. Beneath the dark cliffs, the twisting rocky ravines of Chew and Greenfield Brooks have been flooded with reservoirs that temper their sullen hillscapes with pastel blue. Sailing boats glide across the waters, making full use of the hillside breezes. The ambience attracts many visitors: some to walk round the lake, others to take to the wild hills above.

1 Saddleworth Edges

*At Saddleworth, Black Hill's dark mossy slopes
relent and tumble into the deep gorges of Greenfield
and Chew Brooks. They do so in spectacular
fashion, with the Edges' rocky cliffs and boulder
slopes looking down on a pleasant valley filled with
blue reservoirs, woodland and green fields. Although
the area around the lakes may be teeming with
tourists, the walker will leave many behind where
the dark slopes and the Ravenstones close in and
the path gets ready to strike for the hills.*

Distance: 8 miles/13km	Not recommended in wintry conditions.
Height gain: 1,050ft/320m	**Start/Finish:** Binn Green car park. GR018042.
Walking time: 4/5 hours	**Note:** The walk uses access areas which may be closed on a few days between August 12 and December 10 (not Sundays) or at times of high fire risk.
Type of walk: A boulder-hopping scramble to the moorland edge then easy going following the top edge of gritstone precipices.	

Descend the flight of steps from the car park
through spruce woods to the reservoir road, turning
left past the Yeoman Hey dam and along the shore

of the reservoir beneath Bill o' Jack's plantation.

William Bradbury, nicknamed Bill o' Jack, owned the now-demolished Moorcock Inn. In 1832 he and his father John met their death at the hands of brutal murderers. The assailants were never brought to justice.

Follow the track as it climbs past the Greenfield dam before continuing beyond the reservoir and alongside Greenfield Brook.

The powerful stream bounds over its bed of boulders in a series of cataracts. The drama that lies ahead begins to unfold as the savage ravine narrows and hillsides draw close. A prominent pillar, the Trinnacle, appears on the fringe of the Ravenstones Edge.

Cross the footbridge and continue on the southern banks of Greenfield Brook. The watercourses divide beneath the bouldered lower slopes of Middle Edge Moss. Holme Clough, an interesting rocky gorge that is unfortunately out of bounds, delves into the inner sanctuary of Black Hill's marshes, but this route follows Birchen Clough. First it climbs above the entrance to an aqueduct that steals the water of the clough and pumps it into Dovestone Reservoir.

The route from here is a bit of a scramble and the path threads between and hops over boulders. It crosses and recrosses the stream but becomes less obvious on the narrow craggy approaches to some waterfalls. Leave the intermittent path above these falls and scramble up the western hill slopes to gain a well-used path that doubles back along the edges above Ravenstones.

This time there is a bird's-eye view of the confluence of the Birchen and Holme cloughs with the Sail Bark rocks on Lamb Knoll vying for attention amongst some of the most rugged moor and glen scenery of the Dark Peak. Looking inland a great tract of mossland swells to Black Hill. The walker is reassured that he is somewhat luckier than those Pennine Wayfarers struggling somewhere up there with only the thought of a bacon sandwich at Snoopy's snack van keeping them from turning back.

The path arcs left, high above Greenfield Brook and

its reservoir. The Trinnacle, a great split pillar of gritstone, captures centre-stage hereabouts. Those with a head for heights may not be able to resist the challenge of a climb to its exposed perch before continuing along the edge above Ravenstones.

There is a narrow path cutting across the moor to the left via Major's Cairn (Major was a dog), but the finest route hugs the edge, rounding the corner above the Ashway Rocks, which overlook Yeoman Hey Reservoir and its surrounding woods.

The path passes to the west of an ornate stone cross that commemorated the death of MP James Platt, who was killed in a shooting accident in 1857. Platt's brother once owned Ashway Gap House, a Victorian castellated mansion, which stood at the foot of Dovestone Clough until it was demolished by the old water authority in the 1960s.

After passing the rocky platform known as the Ashway Stone, the wide path narrows and rounds Ashway Gap, where it flounders a little in the mosses that surround the upper reaches of Dovestone Clough and its side streams. Ignore the right of way marked on the maps. It takes you across the peaty mosses without the consolation of being on the tops. Instead keep with the narrow path round the top of the gap.

The path regains its composure on more rocky edges, first the Dean Rocks, then the Great Dove Stone Rocks. The cairn on Fox Stone commemorates two young climbers who, in 1972, fell to their deaths in the Dolomites. Continuing over rocks and a little heather, the path comes to Bramley's Cot, the curious remains of a shooters' hut built into the cliff's edge. The groove where the roof would have been attached is still visible.

By now the largest of the three reservoirs, Dovestone, is in full view, crammed between craggy hilltops at the head of a pastured valley dotted with the mills of Greenfield. Often sailing boats will be gliding across the waters, adding a serenity to the scene. Gradually the hollow below narrows and the fields recede to rough pastures of the Chew Valley, which, in their turn, transform into a rugged scything ravine full of boulders and rimmed with crag.

The Dish Stone has been likened both to a mushroom and a pile of dishes. The huge outcrop looks down on a metalled lane that has climbed from the valley. More often than not many walkers, looking like ants from this viewpoint, will be climbing on this unadventurous course to the Chew Reservoir, which, at 1,607ft/490m, was once England's highest – that accolade now belongs to Cow Green Reservoir in the North Pennines, though it's close. If the people of the North East get thirsty the title will revert.

The path descends to the lane by a little quarry where the stone for the Chew dam was hewn. Follow the road down the clough, watching out for the path which at GR025024 descends to cross Chew Brook on a little footbridge before climbing via some steps by its far banks. The path contours the rough slopes of Stable Stones, crosses Rams Clough and enters Chew Piece Plantation via a ladder stile. It continues high in the woods, which are a pleasant mix of oak, sycamore rowan and ash. High in the skyline the Wimberry Stones, a favourite with climbers, fringe the bouldery hills.

After leaving the woods the path fords a stream, using some stepping stones, and heads across boulder-strewn terrain to a pine plantation, which it enters by a gate. Turn right to descend by a stream at an open corner of the forest (GR007033). Cross to the west bank on leaving the forest and go through a gap in the bottom wall to reach the lane opposite the terraced mill-cottages at Hey Top.

Follow the eastbound lane, which swings left to pass beneath the grass-covered Dovestone Dam. Climb out on the footpath at its northern end, tracing the reservoir's shoreline. On reaching Binn Green's sprucewoods climb the courtesy footpath back to the car park.

2 Black Hill and Laddow

Seen from the depths of Longdendale, Black Hill and its infamous mires hide behind Hey Edge's mantle of green. The shy hill only reveals itself from Laddow Rocks, even then saving its true colours until those final footsteps across the peat plateau. The Pennine Way approach from Crowden is the most popular route to the summit, tracing the winding valley of Crowden Great Brook and passing the impressive Laddow Rocks before that final pull to the summit.

Distance:
9 miles/14km
Height gain:
1,310ft/400m
Walking time:
5/6 hours
Type of walk:
A strenuous moorland walk requiring good navigational abilities. Save this one for summer or crisp winter days when the ground would be hard with frost.
Start/Finish:
Car park, Crowden. GR073994.

A path from the back of Crowden's car park leads past the toilet block and the campsite to a crossroads of tracks. Turn left on a tarred lane, which degenerates into a stony lane beyond a one-arched stone bridge across Crowden Brook. Just before reaching a pine wood turn right on a well-defined path climbing the Crowden valley's western flanks through rough grasslands. The

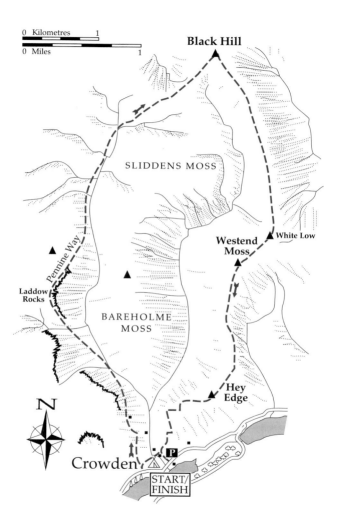

Black Hill

SLIDDENS MOSS

Pennine Way

Laddow Rocks

Westend Moss

White Low

BAREHOLME MOSS

Hey Edge

N

Crowden

START/FINISH

0 Kilometres 1

0 Miles 1

P

sullen gritstone cliffs of Black Tor and Highstone Rocks fringe the skyline.

Beyond the grassy spur of Bareholme Moss, Crowden Brook divides to become Crowden Little and Crowden Great Brooks (east and west respectively), and their valleys bite deep into the surrounding moors and mosses.

The path weaves and undulates among the grassy knolls above Crowden Great Brook. Unfortunately the path improvers have subdued it with great gritstone paving slabs along the section climbing out of the valley to the cliffs.

The path fords Oakenclough Brook before reaching the foot of the Laddow Rocks. These fine gritstone cliffs were once a favourite haunt of climbers but have recently fallen out of favour. Further ascent brings the path to the clifftop, where a well-defined path traces the edge.

A small cairn preceding the highest of the cliffs marks a divergence of paths. Ignore the one to the left, which cuts across Laddow Moss to the Chew Reservoir, but continue on the official Pennine Way, which goes along the crest of the Laddow Rocks for about half a mile (850m) before descending to rejoin the lively Crowden Great Brook.

The path crosses and recrosses the stream many times on its way through rushes and reeds. After leaving the stream, a path inlaid with more heavy gritstone slabs, traverses the drab green expanse of Grains Moss. Black Hill is little more than a mound on the horizon – nothing to fire the imagination.

When the gradient eases to the plateau of Black Hill, the slabs end. The walker has a short section of gravel and peat moss, but is soon faced with terrain as black and devoid of vegetation as anywhere in the British Isles: one that fills Pennine Wayfarers with trepidation – a legacy from a huge peat fire. A concrete trig point juts out from the middle of the morass on a summit known as Soldiers' Lump.

Forsake the Pennine Way for a route heading south-east across the plateau. Go over a stile by a five-bar gate in a wire fence before continuing on a cairned path across a wasteland bereft of vegetation. Beyond that the path continues through the peat-hagged terrain of Tooleyshaw Moss. The summit massif narrows to form a grassy ridge at Tooleyshaw Moor, where the hollow of Heyden Brook can be seen deepening to the left and that of the twisting Crowden Little Brook to the right. The tall Holme Moss radio mast reaches for the sky across Heyden Brook.

On White Low, where cotton grass abounds, the path veers south-west and descends to the edge of the Crowden Little Brook valley. A narrow path follows the edge for a while before dropping through rushes, reeds and cotton grass to meet a wide shooters' track. Follow this beneath the boulder heaps of a disused quarry, where some newly planted woods add a splash of colour to an otherwise steely scene. By now Longdendale has come into view with the rocky northern walls of Bleaklow parading themselves across the valley and its reservoirs.

Abandon the track as it veers left beneath the quarries for a path to the right, descending to a stile before continuing down the hillside above Brockholes Wood. Beyond another stile the path joins a partially paved track that zigzags down to a tarred farm lane. Turn left down the lane to the crossroads by the campsite. Go straight ahead then left by the toilet block back to the car park.

3 Black Hill and Wessenden

The Pennine Way offers two ways northwards off Black Hill. This route uses both: one on the approach, and one for the return, taking in the Wessenden Valley and Black Moss in the process. It crosses a wilderness of peat — places where cotton grass, heather, the odd bilberry and sphagnum moss fight for survival in inhospitable hillscapes. It is a wild walk, a bleak walk, and can be a crowded walk if you take it on a summer Sunday. But try it midweek, say in August, when the heather blooms and see the subtle tweeds of nature beneath your boots and the wide blue sky above your head.

Distance: 9 miles/15km	**Type of walk:** Fairly strenuous walk over peaty moorland.
Height gain: 1,050 ft/320m	**Start/Finish:** Wessenden Head car park. GR077077.
Walking time: 5 hours	

The high car park lies on the Yorkshire side of Black Hill's vast mosses between the heads of the Wessenden Valley and Marsden Clough. Although the route will eventually head south for Black Hill's summit, it looks first at the greenery and lakes of the first mentioned.

It descends on a wide track past Wessenden Head

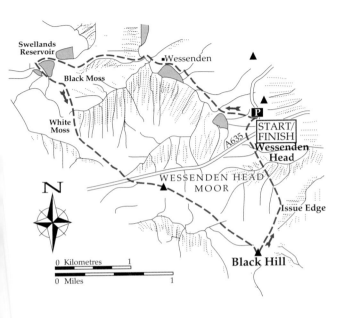

Reservoir and along the shores of the Wessenden Reservoir before swinging left of the large and stately, stone-built Wessenden Lodge.

Abandon the track north of the lodge where a Pennine Way sign points the way down to a small footbridge across Shiny Brook close to its confluence with Blakeley Clough. A narrow path climbs steep banks to a covered water tank that tops the grassy knoll overlooking Blakeley Clough's shady bracken-filled ravine. The perch offers good views northwards across the reservoirs.

The path proceeds with its climb westwards to a weir on Blakeley Clough. Cross the stream just below the weir and climb a narrow grooved path along the northern bank to the lofty expanses of Black Moss, where the bracken recedes to heather, cotton grass and rushes. The path becomes more sketchy as it veers right between Swellands and Black Moss Reservoirs. Beyond the latter it turns sharp left across its dam to traverse the heather-cloaked peaty slopes of Black Moss, descending to cross a couple of cloughs before continuing across Broadhead Moss. Several more cloughs traverse the route before it reaches White Moss.

The derelict rush-filled ditch that bisects White Moss was formerly the Cotton Famine Road, one of many highways built by the cotton workers who were made redundant by the lack of raw material during the American Civil War.

The next section of the route was once the worst of the whole Pennine Way, a morass of oozing peat bog, worn into submission by walkers' boots. One look at the terrain either side of the path gives the walker a hint of past conditions, but it is only a hint – they were much worse!

If you are lucky Snoopy will have parked his van by the busy A635 that straddles the Pennine watershed between Oldham and Holmfirth. He does a rather good bacon and egg sandwich and large mugs of tea. If you are unlucky, then you get an early start to the plod up Black Hill.

Current maps show the Pennine Way starting across the road, but, in fact, the line shown is trackless and unacceptably rough. It is much easier to turn left and follow roadside verges for 300yds/m to an old quarry track (GR054064 – marked by a footpath signpost). The track degenerates into a peaty path that climbs steadily south-east across Dean Head Moss. On the approach to Black Hill's summit massif, the vegetation gets thinner, and the last steps to the trig point on Soldiers' Lump are across naked peat.

The route descends north-eastwards from Black Hill's summit on a cairned course across the bare peat. The situation soon improves, however, and the terrain becomes firm once more.

The chasm of Issue Clough lends shape to the landscape; something that has been missing for a while. Except in dry spells the waters of the clough cascade between shaly slopes in a spout-like waterfall. Beyond it the more verdant rolling pastures lead the eye to Holmfirth, where scenes from Last of the Summer Wine *are shot. Beyond Issue Clough the cairned path offers wider views with the cities of Yorkshire sprawled across the horizon.*

The path veers northwards before meeting and following a straight boundary ditch straddling the lower moors and three more cloughs en route to the busy A635 road at Wessenden Head. Often an ice cream/hot dog van lies in wait for the hungry walker and passing motorists. Although it is a welcome sight for flagging spirits there are no excuses – the car lies just down the road.

4 Black Hill and Holme Moss

This isn't a route for the connoisseur, but it is the quickest way to Black Hill: one that requires the least effort and one of the drier approaches too. It can be done after tea on a summer evening, but make sure there are enough light hours left for the tricky return over Heyden Brook.

Distance:
3³/₄miles/6km
Height gain:
425 ft/130m
Walking time:
2 hours (in dry summer months, else 3 hours)
Type of walk:
Easy moorland stroll or hill run in summer, but with a sting in the tail. Care needed on the descent to Heyden Brook.
Start/Finish:
Car park, Holme Moss. GR097038.
Note:
The walk uses access areas, which may be closed on a few days between August 12 and December 10 (not Sundays) or at times of high fire risk.

Head south-west from the car park along the roadside to the first corner. Here turn right and follow the brow high above Heyden Brook. A sheeptrack on short grassy terrain avoids all the hassle of the peat groughs lying to the east.

The deep chasm of the brook leads the eye to the crinkled peat-hagged top of Black Hill, which fills the

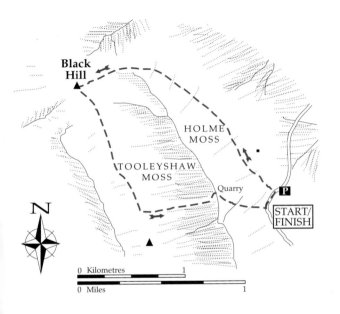

horizon ahead. Heyden Brook shallows and, with its attendant fence, veers west. The path follows suit, and uses a convenient wide channel through the peat moors. By following the meandering channel, the trig point at Soldiers' Lump appears, but only at the last minute.

As it is a short route there may be some time for exploration. The head of Issue Clough probably offers the best refreshment stop, for there are a few rocks on which to sit and admire the views across shaly slopes to the Yorkshire plains.

The way down from Soldier's Lump is trackless at first. Aim south-east. A gate in the fence appears across the peat groughs. Beyond a stile to its right, a cairned path goes across ground bereft of vegetation.

Beyond it the path continues through the peat-hagged terrain of Tooleyshaw Moss. Where the ridge is abandoned is not critical, but, as it narrows, a wide grassy channel to the left marked by a cairn forms a convenient route eastwards into the deep valley of Heyden Brook. The tall Holme Moss radio mast should be straight ahead.

The easier ground of a grassy swathe in the moor, shorn to manageable proportions by sheep, offers an acceptable way down. Otherwise aim for some scabby streamside rocks. They show the position of the quarries where the stream is easiest to ford (the quarries are hidden from this vantage). Note also the position of a faint track that rakes up the opposite side of the valley.

The final descent to Heyden Brook is steep – take care. Once across the brook seek out the track climbing south-east out of the valley across rough grassy slopes. Watch out for the narrow path to the left, highlighted by a post halfway up the hillside. This leads to a stile in the roadside fence at Upper Heyden, a short way south-west of the car park.

Bleaklow

Bleaklow is vast, and vies with the Cross Fell range as the wildest stretch of moorland within England. Anybody who has only seen Bleaklow from the Pennine Way routes could be forgiven for dismissing it as an unattractive swamp, highlighted only by a pair of stones that look as if they are kissing. But the dedicated explorer willing to walk that little bit farther will find that Bleaklow is a wonderful wilderness with many facets and inner secrets.

There is a ridge of sorts. It spans the high ground between Higher Shelf Stones to the west and Barrow Stones in the east. Logically this could be extended to the Derwent Edges, but they are not generally regarded as being part of Bleaklow.

The boggiest terrain lies between the Hern Stones and Bleaklow Stones and at the heads of the watercourses. The skill in plotting a route is in the timing, and by not attempting to go against the grain of the land. The timing is easy: do not go when it's wet or when the cloud hangs low. Working with the grain of the land is harder. Cutting across the deep groughs is a tiring business and it is far better to walk along the line of them. Often, at the heads of the streams and cloughs, the grain alters and the groughs bite deep into the natural ridge line.

Several valleys delve into Bleaklow's heartland. The finest, the Upper Derwent, begins as a reservoir-filled, tree-enshrouded valley and twists and narrows into a remote rock-fringed ravine, cloaked with bracken, heather and swaying moor grasses. It offers a delightful way to the tops, as does the greener valley of Shelf Brook, which conveys the ancient Doctor's Gate Roman road to the moors, and Yellow Slacks.

Through much hard work Bleaklow's walkers should find their remote rocky perch among the heather and bilberry. From there they can quietly watch the world go by.

5 Bleaklow Stones

This is the premier expedition to Bleaklow's heart and is a 'must' for lovers of solitude. It begins in the inky forests by the Derwent Valley reservoirs but quickly escapes to the wide open spaces where heathland studded with crag and boulder stretches for mile upon mile beneath even wider skies.

Distance:
12miles/19km
Height gain:
1,310ft/400m
Walking time:
8 hours
Type of walk:
Strenuous moorland walk requiring the competent use of map and compass.
Start/Finish:
Howden Reservoir car park. GR168938. (On summer weekends or Bank Holidays you must park at Fairholmes by the Derwent Dam and catch a shuttle bus).
Note:
The walk uses access areas, which may be closed on a few days between August 12th and December 10th (not Sundays) or at times of high fire risk.

Take the flinted forest road between the spruce trees and Howden Reservoir to Slippery Stones.

Here the original 17th-century twin-arched bridge that spanned the river at Derwent village was in 1959 reconstructed, stone by stone, after the fund-raising efforts of Sheffield author and journalist, John Derry.

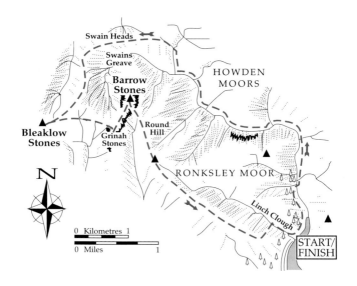

Cross the bridge to follow the stony track along the east side of the river. On leaving the forest behind, the walk enters the wilder environs of the Upper Derwent Valley. The track continues across Cranberry Clough and Broadhead Clough. An attractive waterfall cascades down the latter. Beneath the gritstone crags of Crow Stones Edge the Upper Derwent valley snakes westwards and the path follows suit.

Although more often than not innocuous, the crossing of Stainery Clough can be problematic after heavy rains. It may be necessary to climb higher to make a safe fording. Take care!

Beyond Stainery Clough the woodlands cease. The harsh bare moors that have taken over, are colourful with heather, bracken and the mottled greens of bilberry and moor grass.

The track ends at a marshy plot beyond Lands Clough. Do not be tempted to follow the path too close to the riverbank (it's very boggy). Instead use the sketchy course higher up past Humber Knolls and Coldwell Clough.

At GR144977, a faint path climbs out of the Derwent Valley above the eastern banks of Hoar Clough. A group of rocks known as the Shepherds Meeting Stones crowd the skyline. On reaching them a right of way heads generally northwards to the main watershed. It is, however, better to go west instead across access land, crossing the stream and keeping to the gritstone edges, including Dean Head Stones before reaching the watershed at Swains Head. This way the worst of the marshy peat hags of Featherbed Moss can be avoided.

A series of stakes guides the walker across a wide ridge, veering south, then south-west. The wet path meanders round the innumerable cloughs of yet another Featherbed Moss and the deeper hollow of the Westend Valley before finally stumbling upon terra firma at Bleaklow Stones.

This fine perch is adorned by more gritstone than peat, and fine gritstone it is too! The Anvil and the Trident are just two of the natural sculptures that stimulate the imagination. The stony escarpment ends at Grinah Stones, which looks down on declining moorland where the chocolate and biscuit of the heather and tussocky grass is divided by the pallid green tentacles of the Westend Valley and its side cloughs.

Grinah Stones, which lies to the east, is the next port of call. Instead of crossing the expected sea of peat, the walker can get there on a narrow but good path, which descends slightly, encircling the brow of the hillside above Deep Grain. The nooks and crannies in Grinah Stone's bold gritstone outcrops offer good shelter for those caught out in hostile conditions and it is maybe a good place for lunch.

A narrow path across the heather heads north-east to Barrow Stones, where the rocks are more scattered across the hillside, but interesting to those with an eye for the weird, especially when the mists swirl. The summit overlooks the Upper Derwent valley and the stony escarpments of Howden Edge dominate the scene.

Follow the path from Barrow Stones, heading south-east across more heather to the wind shelter and rocks on Round Hill. It descends to some wet ground and joins a shooters' track that has climbed from Westend. Hereabouts a shallow grassy channel, Black Dike, offers an invaluable help down Ridge Nether Moor. It passes a line of shooting butts before turning left. At its termination, scramble down the steep slopes into the shadows of Linch Clough. Here a prominent route crosses the stream before twisting right to enter the spruce plantations of Upper Wood, where a good track drops to the forestry road just north of the car park.

6 Bleaklow

Looking away from the line of pylons, the reservoirs and the roads to the crusty rocks of Bleaklow's northern edge and the smoother-profiled hillsides to the north it is obvious that Longdendale once was a beautiful if rugged valley. Just five minutes from the roadside a fascinating wilderness awaits and this long, tough circular route takes up the challenge. It leads the walker along an attractive crag-lined mountain clough to Bleaklow's inner sanctum, a place covered with mosses, huge peat groughs, a little heather and gritstone outcrop.

Distance:
12 miles/19km
Height gain:
1,805ft/505m
Walking time:
7/8 hours
Type of walk:
Strenuous. A high moorland walk crossing many wet peaty areas. It is best left to the early summer months or winter days when the frost or snow has hardened the peat. For experienced walkers with good map and compass skills.
Start/Finish:
Roadside car park near Woodhead Tunnel. GR112999.
Note:
Parts of the route can be closed on shooting days between August 12 and December 10 and at times of high fire risk.

The Woodhead Tunnel, which used to convey the Manchester to Sheffield Railway for nearly 4 miles (6km) beneath the moors, lies boarded up and redundant, the last reminders of industry before the trek to the moors.

Follow the track from the roadside car park down to the River Etherow and across the bridge to the southern bank. The well-used path continues eastwards by some pleasant woodland at Birchen Bank before turning southwards into Black Clough. Leave the track and ford the stream at GR117995 using convenient boulders as stepping stones. A shooters' track now winds round to climb the scrub-covered banks of an old quarry.

Black Clough divides into three, providing the heather-clad moors with attractive rocky tree-filled ravines. The track continues its climb above the east banks of Far Black Clough.

Gritstone crags line this busy little stream and the odd wind-lashed tree adds an extra splash of colour to the scene. In retrospective views the miry wilderness that is Black Hill masquerades as a pleasant grassy hill, rising gently from the valley below.

The path fades to become little more than a groove in the heather, and the clough shallows, its stream now a mere trickle. Where it gives up, follow one of the little cloughs, all of which will lead to the main Bleaklow 'ridge'.

A spasmodic line of stakes marks the route across this curving, miry watershed. Barrow Stones, a

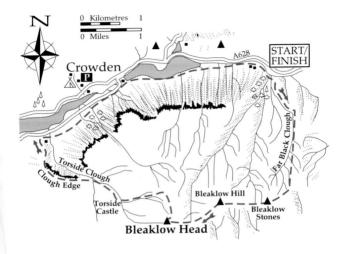

boulder-topped hill, captures much of the attention, rising from the hollow of the Upper Derwent valley, but the watershed route aims for the more distant serrated top of Bleaklow Stones.

It is hard going, but this high and remote top is crusted with some weirdly-shaped weather-sculptured rocks, like the Anvil. Beyond the Stones the stakes persist, but the going gets rougher. It is guaranteed to test the walker's resolve.

Although little more than a mile to Bleaklow Head, the distance blurs and time and effort take over. Although now and then the path finds a gravel-bottomed grough heading in the right direction, the grain of the land generally works against this convenience. Finding the cairn on the summit marked on the map as Bleaklow Hill is unimportant: getting to Bleaklow Head is all.

Marked by a tall post and small stone cairn, Bleaklow Head is usually the congregation point of walkers who have braved Bleaklow, many through that avenue of mud, the Devil's Dyke. From the Head, the heathery eastern flanks of the hill decline to the Etherow Valley while Black Hill and the line of cliffs known as Laddow Rocks complete the picture.

All is downhill to Crowden – and it is much drier too. Cairns mark the way off the top and a faint path traverses peatlands to the heathery terrain above Wild Boar Grain. The path follows the northern rim of the grain and eventually fords it close to its confluence with an unnamed stream near the John Track Well (spring) – GR081964. The deepening defile is joined by Torside Grain and transforms into Torside Clough, a cavernous crag-studded gorge.

The path, now distinct, follows the high edge of the clough which, as it veers to the north, opens out into the valley of Longdendale. Black Hill's southern flanks fill the skyline across the Torside Reservoir and those pylons remind the walker that civilisation is near to hand.

The path plummets on precipitous grassy slopes towards Reaps Farm. Leave it at GR064977 at an intersection with a grassy track that doubles back into the depths of the clough to ford its stream close to the inlet of a leat. The leat conveys water for nearly three miles to a couple of small reservoirs above Padfield.

A narrow path climbs northwards out of the clough. Turn left on meeting another narrow path. This clambers over boulder-strewn slopes beneath Long Gutter Edge before veering left to descend past some woodland towards the Torside Information Centre.

For those in need of sustenance, there may be a mobile refreshment van waiting in the car park. Otherwise turn right before reaching the car park and follow the trackbed of a disused railway that, until its closure in 1981, linked Manchester and Sheffield via the Woodhead Tunnel. It now serves as a recreational path, the Longdendale Trail, between Hadfield and Windle Edge.

The shaly trackbed, passing beneath the dark, crag-rimmed slopes of Northern Bleaklow, takes the walk all the way back to the car park at the Woodhead Tunnel.

7 Higher Shelf Stones and Doctor's Gate

When Bleaklow comes to mind, peat groughs, sinking limbs and muddy boots are not far behind. The most popular approach along Devil's Dike and the Pennine Way reveals little shape to the hill. It's an exercise in damage limitation on swelling moorland porridge. Viewed from the west, however, Bleaklow shows some rocks and a distinctive profile: perhaps it is a true mountain after all. The approach from Old Glossop is the finest and, although there are the infamous peat hags, walkers will march through them on firm channels.

Distance:
7 miles/11km
Height gain:
1,510ft/460m
Walking time:
4/5 hours
Type of walk:
Strenuous moorland walk, that occasionally leaves recognised footpaths. It requires the competent use of map and compass.
Start/Finish:
Old Glossop.
GR043947.

Transport:
GMS bus No 215 from Manchester Piccadilly (via Denton, Belle Vue and Hyde) goes right to the start of the walk at the end of Shepley Street.
Note:
The walk uses access areas which may be closed on a few days between August 12 and December 10 (not Sundays) or at times of high fire risk.

Follow Shepley Street eastwards past the factory to the bus turning circle at its terminus. Here a farm track continues in the same direction taking the route into a pleasant rural glen. The partially wooded dome of Shire Hill rises on one side facing the pine and oak-clad slopes of Edge Plantation on the other.

Leave the track for a signposted footpath beginning at a ladder-stile (GR053950). Confined at first by a fence and drystone wall, it climbs north-east across pastureland overlooking the curiously-named but pleasant craggy valley of Shittern Clough. Beyond a second ladder-stile the well-defined path continues on the bilberry-clad moorland spur of Lightside (not named on Landranger maps).

As the path gains height, Kinder Scout's jagged profile peeps out from behind Mill Hill while beneath them both, the Snake Road weaves across the dark heather moors and mosses.

Heather replaces bilberry on upper Lightside and the path becomes one of those delightful stony ribbons that used to proliferate in the Dark Peak before the popularity of hillwalking took its toll. The little path joins the spur's southern edge and suddenly the vast hollow carved by Yellowslacks Brook yawns below.

A dilapidated wire fence joins in from the right and the path goes along the right side of it before joining the cliff edges of Yellow Slacks and the Dog Rock.

The amphitheatre of gritstone proves to be more spectacular than the map suggests. Across the hollow, Bleaklow's rocky southern escarpment looks every bit a mountain, soaring in crag-fringed waves from Shelf Benches, to James's Thorn, and then higher to Higher Shelf Stones. The view would surprise those who know only the dull Pennine Way plod from the Snake Road.

The path continues along the rocky fringes. The crags close in to form the rugged channel of Dowstone Clough, which eats into the increasingly peaty Bleaklow mosses. Its stream, a trickle in summer but quite boisterous in winter, flows over a solid bed of stone slabs and steps with heathered flanks. The best path stays close to the stream and away from the peat hags that lie to the right.

Eventually the clough shallows and the stream divides among a bed of rushes (GR089954). Head for Higher Shelf Stones by crossing the main stream and following its southbound tributary. For much of the year its course will be dry and most of the bootprints will trace its sandy bed, which, wending through a complex of peat hags, heads generally in a southerly direction. The hags restrict the view, but the walker can rectify this by climbing out on to one of them.

Near the summit the channel shallows and widens giving views of neighbouring fells. Suddenly, the trig point rises from a grassy plinth ahead, then some rocks appear.

Higher Shelf Stones is the finest place on Bleaklow. It's where the tide of peat has been turned back, a place where the visitor can stand on terra firma to view the world. Looking north and east the endless rolling peat moors that characterise Bleaklow are broken by shadowy valleys and the bouldery ramparts of Grinah Stones and Alport Castles. Kinder Scout's crusty northern end repeats the theme to the south. The best views lie to the west. Here, beyond the summit boulders, smooth grassy slopes plummet into the chasm of Shelf Brook. Across the way the buttresses of Lower Shelf Stones and the twisting Doctor's Gate path both direct the gaze to Glossop, which basks amid lower hills. Cracken Edge, Shining Tor and the wide blue plains of Greater Manchester complete the panorama.

The Doctor's Gate path will lead the route back to Old Glossop, but it's a long way down yet. A direct descent would necessitate the crossing of Shelf Brook and a certain amount of re-ascent. It is better to join it beneath Shelf Moor where it crosses to join the northern banks. Contour round the corrie towards Lower Shelf Stones and James's Thorn but circumvent the naked peat to the left. The secret of this descent is to locate the prominent grassy channel that runs just north of west and forms a reliable and reasonably dry course down Shelf Moor. The views are enlivened by Laddow Rocks, a line of cliffs threading deeply into Black Hill.

A little stream runs along the channel in the later stages and together they lead to a boulder-strewn edge above Ferny Hole. There are no real paths from now on, but the routes are quite straight-forward with two alternative ways of getting down to the Doctor's Gate path at GR073942. The shortest rakes down to the grassy shelf to the west of James's Thorn, passing a small pool (marked only on Harvey's Superwalker map) before descending steep grassy flanks parallel to Little Clough (not named on the Landranger map). The other alternative takes in James's Thorn, another good viewpoint or brew point. It is a simple matter of raking up slopes to the left.

A small monument and a small pile of wreckage on the summit mark the place where, on the 18 May 1945, an Avro Lancaster bomber from the Canadian 103 Squadron crashed, killing its crew of seven.

Descend southwards (no real path) from the summit, taking care to avoid the crags and the steepest of the hill slopes. The spur veers gradually south-west, ending abruptly at more crags overlooking Shelf Brook. Doctor's Gate can be seen meandering through the valley below. To join it, turn westwards, then follow the line of Little Clough down to the valley.

Doctor's Gate leads the route westwards alongside the rushing brook. In stark contrast, the hillsides to the left are dark with heather, while those to the right are green with sheep-shorn grass. The path becomes a track; fields and wooded hillsides replace the moors and the walker returns past the factory into Old Glossop, hopefully with dry boots and socks.

8 The Bleaklow Edges of Longdendale

Sometimes the sum of the sides of a mountain amounts to more entertainment than the sum of the tops. For views, the northern edges of Bleaklow are a treat and illustrate perfectly that all on the mountain is not bog.

Distance:
7 miles/11km
Height gain:
1,150ft/340m
Walking time:
4 hours
Type of walk: steep gradients, to high moorland edges, across heather and tussocky moorland, pathless at times but with a fast return on an old railway trackbed.
Start/Finish:
Torside Visitor Centre car park. GR068983.
Note: The walk uses access areas which may be closed on a few days between August 12 and December 10 (not Sundays) or at times of high fire risk.

Longdendale's five reservoirs were constructed to supply Manchester's ever-increasing industries with water in the second half of the 19th century.

A path from the back of the information centre car park leads to the trackbed of an old railway line that, until its closure in 1981, linked Manchester and Sheffield through the Woodhead Tunnel. Cross the railway and go through the gate at the other side. A path through an agreed access area climbs steeply

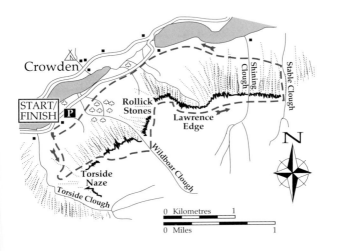

through tussock grassland and passes some woods. It veers right beneath the rocks of Long Gutter Edge and to the rim of Torside Clough.

Across the stream the dark cliffs of Clough Edge tower above the scything ravine. Pennine Wayfarers may be seen as shadowy figures walking on its crest.

Do not be tempted by the path descending into the clough, but continue on the one veering left and high above the boisterous stream. Leave the ever-diminishing path for the groove of an old quarry track that climbs the hillside to the left. It reaches a flattish grassy area between Long Gutter Edge (left) and Torside Naze (right). Keep to the foot of the latter.

A fence declines to meet this course. Cross it using the simple stile before climbing the bouldery slopes of White Mare. Strike out eastward across moorland to the deep rocky ravine of Wildboar Clough, which is protected by a wire fence.

Just below the level of the stile to be used, the Rollick Stones arc round a huge boulder field, the remains of an old quarry. Across the reservoirs of Longdendale the rippled cliffs and crags of Laddow Rocks fringe the Crowden Great Brook ravine, one of two that delve from here into the wide expanses of Black Hill.

Follow the fence inland until the ravine shallows enough for a safe crossing. The crossing point will vary depending on the season, the weather and how much water flows in the brook. Once across follow a little path back along the opposite side of the clough, then veer right on the path above Rollick Stones. The route near the Stones is generally pathless, but follows a line between a stone-strewn but rather undefined edge and the peat hags of Shining Clough Moss.

Once across Fair Vage Clough, the path becomes more ingrained on the terrain, and twists amongst bilberry and heather above Lawrence Edge before rounding Deer Knowl. It then diverts right to cross the narrow but deep and rocky cleft of Shining Clough. The stream, which tumbles down a stepped bed of solid rock, requires careful fording when in spate.

Over the water the path resumes, tracing the

opposite banks of the clough back to the edge, where climbers may be practising their skills on the impressive buttresses of the Dowstone Rocks.

At Stable Clough the path comes across a new fence, which should be followed uphill to a stile allowing access to a bulldozed track. Follow this downhill beneath the climbers' crags to a gate on the edge of rough pastures. Turn left, following the fence along wet tussocky ground beneath heather slopes. The path fords Shining Clough by a very marshy route. Two stiles and good waymarking highlight the next section, which sees the route dog-legging to the right, then circumvent a pool lined by rhododendron bushes. A narrow track then traverses rough pasture to reach the access track to The Lodge.

Turn left along the track to the disused cottages of the old Crowden Railway Station, then turn on to the old railway line, following it westwards back to the Torside Visitor Centre.

9 Crowden's Rocks

Some routes surprise you. Longdendale isn't the prettiest of the Peak's valleys, although it does have some good crags, and when the route goes through forest, the dreaded Sitka spruce comes to mind. On this route, however, the largest section of forest has a delicate mixture of broadleaved and coniferous trees with enough space between them to allow some attractive undergrowth. The paths twist and turn beneath and above the crags and outcrops; through heather, over grasslands and mosses, giving lofty views of Longdendale, which is somehow seen in a kinder light.

Distance:
8 miles/13km
Height gain:
1,380 ft/420m
Walking time:
4/5 hours
Type of walk:
Mainly on good tracks and paths with a rough section between High Stone Rocks and Laddow Rocks on

sheep tracks.
Start/Finish:
Car park, Crowden.
GR073994.
Note:
The walk uses access areas which may be closed on a few days between August 12 and December 10 (not Sundays) or at times of high fire risk.

Follow the path from the back of Crowden's car park past the toilet block and the campsite. Turn

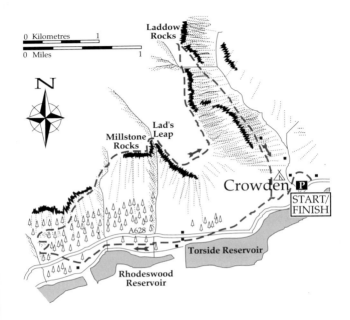

left at the crossroads of tracks on a tarred lane, which degenerates into a stony lane beyond a one-arched stone bridge across Crowden Brook.

After climbing across rough pastureland, the walled lane passes a small plantation of pine. It reveals good views across Torside Reservoir and the deep scything ravine of Torside Clough across the far shores.

The lane descends to the busy A628 road. Cross the road with care to the path immediately opposite, which descends to a strip of woodland fringing the reservoir. Turn right along the path, tracing the northern shores of the reservoir. Beyond a gate it veers left to the dam. Don't cross, but follow the track above the shoreline of the Rhodeswood Reservoir. The waymarked route goes through the left of two gates passing through scrubland to the dam, where a tarred lane climbs through woodland back to the road.

The next track lies across the road, staggered to the left. It zigzags up slopes dappled with heather before entering some delightful woods where oak, birch, larch and pine are mixed with open patches of heather and bilberry, studded with boulders. The track climbs steadily to the skyline giving increasingly good lofty views of Longdendale's lakes and gritstone edges.

The path reaches the moors by Rawkins Brook, a deep-set watercourse that plummets down to the valley in a series of boisterous falls. Cross the stile in the fence and follow a peaty path north-eastwards across the heather moor towards the bouldered edge of the Millstone Rocks. There has been a certain amount of land slippage on the first rocks encountered and it would be wise not to get too close to the edge.

At Lad's Leap, the Hollins Clough stream dives from its slabbed rocky bed into Coombes Clough. I doubt very much if any lad could leap the rocks across this gap. Mere mortals descend in the normal manner to ford the stream and climb out and along the moorland to the east.

An intermittent and dilapidated wall comes in from the right and the path begins its decline towards the Crowden Valley. Because this route visits Laddow Rocks before returning to Crowden, it is unnecessary to descend into the valley.

Where the path begins a steeper descent towards a moorland plinth above the valley (a cairn marks the spot), leave it and head northwards towards Rakes Rocks, following the thinnest of sheep tracks along the moorland rim. Just as they look like running out, new tracks begin. A couple of small cairns give the walker increased confidence in the route and soon Rakes Rocks are achieved. The crags are dark and vegetated and look down on the Pennine Way climbing from Crowden Great Brook across a series of grassy knolls.

The deep hollow of Oakenclough Brook makes for an interesting crossing and the terrain gets a bit rougher, but shortly beyond it the route joins the slabbed Pennine Way route on its climb to the top of Laddow Rocks. The fine gritstone cliffs were once popular with climbers but not so much nowadays.

The Pennine Way route offers the best way back to Crowden. Descend south along the slabbed path, to ford Oakenclough Brook lower down than before. It is easier here too. The Way undulates over the grassy knolls beneath Rakes Rocks and Black Tor before descending to the walled lane used on the outward route (GR068991). Retrace the route, descending to the bridge over Crowden Brook and pass the campsite and toilet block back to the car park.

10 Alport Castles

Alport Dale is but a short dale with no motor roads and a scant population. Although it explores the inner recesses of Bleaklow it would have few devotees were it not for its famous castles, a huge area of landslip where gritstone surfaces like rows of teeth. The castles can be combined with a remote route to Bleaklow and Grains-in-the-Water, but this circular route from Fairholmes in the Derwent Valley makes a pleasing change from a moorland yomp.

Distance: 8 miles/13km	*Start/Finish:* Fairholmes Information Centre. GR173893.
Height gain: 2,000ft/610m	*Note:* The walk is over a permitted access area, which can be closed on shooting days between August 12 and December 10 and also at times of high fire risk.
Walking time: 5 hours	
Type of walk: A strenuous moorland and forestry walk with lots of ups and downs.	

The route begins from the roadside opposite the car park on a permissive forestry track that is sign-posted to Lockerbrook. It climbs through the conifers of Hagg Side Wood, crossing the bridge over an artificial watercourse before steepening. Some beech and birch trees mingle with the spruce

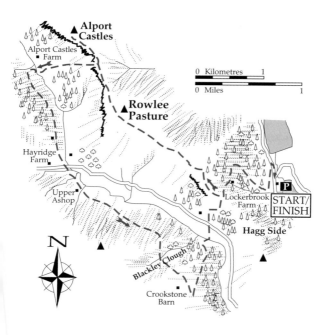

and pines. Near the top the waymarked path turns right then left to leave the forest for the high pastures north-east of Lockerbrook Farm. A clear path crosses the fields guided by a stone wall. Turn left at the top signpost and follow a track south past the Lockerbrook Farm and along the top edge of the Hagg Side plantations.

At the ridge-top by Woodcock Coppice, turn right to climb along a permissive path. Beyond two stiles in intervening walls the path enters open moorland

and climbs past the rocks of Bellhag Tor, which overlook a huge landslide.

Views across the Woodlands Valley include Kinder Scout's northern edges, where the rocks of Blackden Clough and the angular cliffs known as The Chinese Wall (not named on the map) are studded onto a backdrop of rough dark moorland.

The path climbs steadily, over the hump of Rowlee Pasture, beyond which a crumbling drystone wall breaks the simplicity of the hillscape. The route now looks down on a new valley, that of the Alport. Hereabouts it is a mixture of farm, pasture and forest, but transforms into a wild, twisting moorland gorge in its upper reaches.

Beyond the wall, Alport Castles look down on the valley. Tiered gritstone crags and a tor, The Tower, rise from a huge chaotic jumble of loose boulders and grassy mounds high on the hillside. It's all part of what is believed to be the biggest landslip in the country. The crags are still extremely unstable and climbing would be foolhardy.

A good path descends from the southern end of the castles. In reality this path follows the OS Outdoor Leisure map's black dotted line rather than the parallel green right of way line. In the early stages it follows an old drystone wall: in the lower regions it traces the perimeter of Alport Castles wood.

After crossing the footbridge over the river, the path veers right over rough riverside meadows to Alport Castle Farm, where a track swings round to nearby Alport Farm. Here the track leads southwards down the valley beneath spruce trees and pastureland.

Where the track veers right towards Hayridge Farm, abandon it for a signposted footpath that descends south-east across a meadow, to cross another stile in a stone wall at the edge of a small wood. The path stays above the riverbanks to exit on the busy Snake road.

Across the road follow a track that leads to a ford across the River Ashop. A nearby footbridge allows a drier crossing of the river. Rejoin the track and follow it eastwards, skirting the hill slopes beneath Upper Ashop Farm.

The grooved track, which is part of a Roman road linking forts near Glossop and Bradwell, climbs steadily across the rough grassy slopes of Blackley Hey. Ignore the left fork descending to Rowlee Bridge, but continue the climb on slopes now clad with bilberry, crowberry and heather. After rounding Blackley Clough the ancient highway descends to the crossroads east of Crookstone Barn (GR159877).

By now the western finger of Ladybower Reservoir can be seen, stretching between the forests of the Woodlands Valley.

Turn left on a rutted track that becomes a sunken track descending along the top edge of the pine woods before entering into the darkness beneath its canopy of spruce and fir. The track, now a damp stony one, should be abandoned shortly after a right-hand bend for a narrow path, which starts by a small stream. It descends through the woods before veering right to cross the River Ashop at Haggwater Bridge.

On the far banks it climbs steeply through more pleasant mixed woodland to the A57 Snake road. Immediately opposite, a track climbs out of the valley to the east of Hagg Farm and zigzags across the upper slopes at the edge of Woodcock Coppice before skirting the Hagg Side conifer plantations. Here retrace earlier steps back to the car park, making sure not to miss the 'Fairholmes' sign-posted route, just north of the Lockerbrook farm.

Kinder Scout and Edale

One look at the map will show that Kinder Scout is no ordinary hill. Strangely angular, its slopes end in abrupt edges. An almost flat summit is indented with a network of small watercourses resembling a diagram of the human nervous system.

More often than not the watercourses have no water in them, but form a horrendous network of sticky peat groughs. Outside the summer months only masochists and the most intrepid of bog trotters would enjoy a walk on the plateau.

That said, Kinder Scout is the most popular of the Dark Peak destinations. The fact that it has no real summit means that the walker feels the mountain has been conquered the moment the plateau is gained. He or she can then enjoy the promenade along the gritstone edges taking in the views and exploring the weird world of weathered rocky tors and outcrops.

The southern and western edges above Hayfield and Edale have always been the more popular and that leaves the northern and eastern confines to those who like their hills less crowded. The approaches by way of Fair Brook and Blackden Brook are particularly rewarding.

A very different group of hills rises on the opposite side of Edale. Greener and more pronounced in form, the Great Ridge invites many walkers to its tops, which include Lose Hill, Mam Tor and Lord's

Seat. From any one of them Kinder Scout's serrated southern facade can be seen to perfection rising from the chequered fields of the valley. The walking is easier and high car parks make it more accessible to the casual walker. This, combined with the soft friable shales of its make-up, mean that the paths have been badly eroded. When walking on the ridge be conscious that these are very vulnerable hills.

I have not included any walks to Mam Tor itself. The stone inlaid summit is artificial and too close to those roadside car parks to be of any significance to anyone but the peak-bagger.

11 Blackden and Seal Edges

Following the same ancient highways used by packhorse trains and Roman legions, this demanding route explores Kinder Scout's eastern edges. It does so both from the fringe of the moor and from across the Woodlands Valley and proves that Kinder Scout has its share of quiet places for those willing to explore that little bit further.

Distance:
12miles/19km
Height gain:
1,575ft/480m
Walking time:
7 hours
Type of walk:
A serious moorland walk with a steady climb on to the ridge followed by peaty paths round the rocky edge and a rough descent to Ashop Clough. Walkers not steady on their feet won't like the plank bridge over the Ashop to the Snake Path.
Start/Finish:
Birchen Clough car park. GR109915.
Note:
The walking is over a permitted access area, which can be closed on shooting days between August 12 and December 10 and also at times of high fire risk.

The path to be used on the initial stages is the course of a Roman road and the continuation of the Doctor's Gate path from Glossop. To reach it follow the Snake Road southwards for 300yds/m. The ancient highway climbs from the left-hand

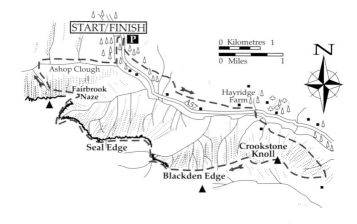

side of its newer counterpart, raking up the hillside through conifer plantations.

As it leaves the forest for open fellside the path on the ground climbs away from the wall and the plantation's top edge rather than by them as suggested on all current maps. However, ignore the left fork, which doubles back to climb north on the upper rim of Oyster Clough. The route to be followed here rejoins the top edge of the plantation at GR115905, then veers right then left, descending by a wall to ford the Oyster Clough stream.

Beyond the stream crossing, the path veers right alongside the wall and fords another little stream. The route now finds itself on a high pastured shelf overlooking the Woodlands Valley. Above and to the left the pastures swell to rough green moorland fringed by the shattered Cowms Rocks. Across the River Ashop, Kinder's rugged Seal Edge crowns hill slopes mottled with bracken, heather and bilberry and broken by the twisting cloughs of Fair Brook and Blackden Brook.

Cross the step stile beyond the ford and follow the prominent path that veers left to run parallel to the Woodlands Valley. Eventually, a wall joins its course and accompanies it down to Hayridge Farm. Just before the farmhouse a waymarker diverts the route diagonally to the left and on to the western side of the Alport Valley. After crossing two stiles the route comes to a wide farm track linking Hayridge and Alport Castles Farm. Take the waymarked footpath heading south-east from the track across a meadow, to cross another stile in a stone wall before threading through woods to the busy Snake road.

The path to Kinder begins on a track across the road. It leads to a ford across the Ashop, but those with an aversion to wet feet should use the nearby footbridge and turn left to rejoin the track, which now heads eastwards skirting the hill slopes. The stony track divides: the one to the right heads for Upper Ashop Farm, but the one used on this occasion continues eastwards, dipping to ford a small brook, before climbing across the slopes of Blackley Hey. Ignore the left fork descending to Rowlee Bridge.

After rounding Blackley Clough, the track meets a gate at the edge of open country (GR158879). Do not go through the gate but follow the worn track westwards on the grassy slopes of Crookstone Hill. The odd tree decorates the austere hillscape while the sparse crags cap the skyline.

A signpost by a tree in the middle of the moor points the way to a stile in the intake wall. Heather replaces much of the grass as the path climbs towards the hilltop, veering left on the upper slopes to thread through the crags. Beyond the higher crags a path doubles back (north-east) to round Crookstone Knoll.

Here the greenery of the Alport valley pierces the pale wastelands of Bleaklow and the ragged edge of Fairbrook Naze juts out behind the smooth rounded slopes of Blackden Moor.

The path divides near some grouse butts a short way east of the knoll. Take the left fork, which gradually curves southwards across heather to some squat gritstone rocks. The path is a short cut for walkers transferring from Kinder's south and north-east edges. Turn right (west) on reaching the rocks on a path that soon discovers some more.

This next and more impressive group are named the Madwoman's Stones. My wife, Nicola, recreated the madwoman in her imagination, but I could not.

The trig point at GR129878 lies directly ahead but follow a little path that heads back across peat groughs to the edge. The edge becomes more defined as the hollow of Blackden Brook opens out, and sleek stone-studded grass slopes flow to the stream, which tumbles in a series of waterfalls from the rock-fringed cliffs down to the Ashop.

After fording several tributaries of the brook, the entertaining path rounds Blackden Moor to the Seal Edge, from where the dark and angular Fairbrook Naze assumes even greater dominance over the landscape. The peat hags of Kinder Scout rarely make incursions this close to the edge and the going is firm. The walk has indeed become a very pleasant promenade with subtly changing views down little cloughs.

The great chunk of gritstone overlooking Fair Brook Clough is known as the Chinese Wall. Beyond it the path turns inland to circumvent Fair Brook Clough, a boulder-strewn ravine biting deeper into the moor than one would expect. After fording the brook, follow the path to the rocks on the top of Fairbrook Naze.

More often than not breezes whistle round the rocks on this exposed promontory, but the views more than compensate. Fairbrook Naze stares across Black Ashop Moor and the Woodlands Valley to the vast moorland sprawl of Bleaklow. Fair Brook wriggles through the high moors of heather and rough grass, the odd tree decorating its wild rock-scattered ravine.

The descent begins down the nose of the promontory from the left side of the rocks. It's steep at first and threads through gaps in the rocks before following an easier course over grass.

Turn left on meeting a faint grassy track that is marked by black dashes on the OS maps. This contours round the moor to the ruins of an old hut lying beneath prominent dark rocks of The Edge. The way down to the footbridge at Ashop Clough (GR091907) is rough and trackless, although a couple of posts mark the way. The best course follows a grassy ribbon by one of the feeder streams. The last drop to the River Ashop is steep and the bridge can be a little unnerving to the unsteady-footed walker, for it turns out to be a heavyweight wooden sleeper spanning two concrete parapets and about six feet (2m) above the watercourse.

On the other side a wide track beginning from an old ruin climbs to the Snake Path, which follows an undulating eastbound course parallel to the river before entering the conifers of the Snake Plantation.

The path exits at the meeting of the River Ashop and Lady Clough's stream. Cross the footbridge over the latter and turn left into Lady Clough. The pleasant streamside walk through spruce and pine crosses a flinted forestry road and continues northwards over a footbridge across Birchen Clough. Turn right beyond the footbridge and climb through the trees to the north of Birchen Clough and into the open where a paved path zigzags and climbs to the Snake road and back to the car park.

12 The Edge and the Snake Path

Kinder Scout's edges all have their share of cliffs, weird outcrops and wide views. Strangely only the southern and western edges, receive widespread attention from hikers. The northern and eastern edges offer relatively quiet walks with the wilderness atmosphere that must have been evident to the early traveller. This route from Woodlands Valley discovers one of the finest little glens on its way to the Seal Edge. After tracing dusky cliffs, it descends to Ashop Head and follows the ancient Snake Path back to base.

Distance:
9miles/15km
Height gain:
1,310ft/400m
Walking time:
5/6 hours
Type of walk:
A serious moorland walk with a steady climbs onto the ridge followed by peaty paths round the rocky edge. Long moorland trek down Ashop Clough.
Start/Finish:
Birchen Clough car park. GR109915.
Note:
The walk is over a permitted access area, which can be closed on shooting days between August 12 and December 10 and at times of high fire risk.

The start of the walk lies directly across the road from the car park. A neat paved path zigzags down grassy banks to a wooden stile at the edge of Snake

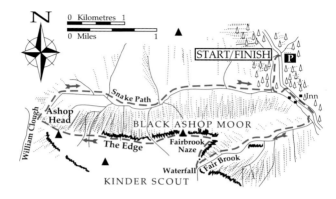

Wood. Descend through the trees into Lady Clough, turning left by the banks of its river to cross a wooden footbridge over a side stream. Continue by the banks of the river, ignoring the concrete bridge conveying a forestry road on to Saukin Ridge.

The path continues south, and the spruce and pine trees thin out to reveal pleasant aspects and an attractive riverside walk. The heather slope of Rough Bank comes into view. Beneath it the clough meets the Woodlands Valley and its river, the Ashop.

Do not cross the footbridge here, that way will be saved for the return route from Ashop Clough. Instead, continue along the riverbank and climb out left on a well-defined path to the Snake Road. The short stretch of road walking brings the route past the popular Snake Inn.

Watch out for the stile on the right marking the start of the footpath at GR115903. The faint path descends to the River Ashop, which it crosses on a wooden footbridge before turning left by a wall to enter the secretive twisting ravine of Fair Brook.

A good path traces the northern banks of the brook and soon enters an enchanting world of waterfalls and crags. Birch and rowan mingle at the streamside, while interlocking spurs dappled with heather and bracken, lead the eye on a merry, twisting dance to the serrated crags of Kinder's Seal Edge.

In the upper reaches scenes become more sullen. Fairbrook Naze and Seal Edge have closed in on the brook. The narrow path is forced into humility and made to sneak through boulderlands to reach Kinder Scout's perimeter path. Double back right to follow the edge route across terrain of gritstone boulder and thick peat to Fairbrook Naze.

From the huge gritstone perches of Fairbrook Naze the wide view encompasses Alport Castles, the Derwent Edges which stretch across the western horizon, and Bleaklow, whose vast expanse fills the northern aspect.

The way along the northern edges carries on in a similar fashion across gritstone and sticky peat. The driest courses are generally nearer the edge, though these could be a little too entertaining for most walkers in mist, ice or wind. A bold track clambers up the edge west of the Naze in equally entertaining fashion: it is part of a Marsden to Edale challenge walk.

On its way westwards along the edge, the route cuts across several streams that tumble from the peat hags of the plateau on to Black Ashop Moor. In summer many will be dry, but after heavy rainfall they will be racing through the rocks.

The path stumbles upon the Boxing Glove Stones, which with a little less imagination than the person who named them, resemble upturned elephants' feet. There are several good perches nearby that would provide an ideal lunch spot. They offer views across Black Ashop Moor, which has become wilder and more shallow. Its pale grassy slopes rise gently to the summit of the Snake road. Beyond, the empty hills rise still farther to Bleaklow, whose wilderness now shares the northern horizon with the Howden Moors.

The northern edge becomes less defined, the precipices become slopes and the rocks less widespread as Kinder Scout's north-western corner nears. Rather than just descending directly to Ashop Head, take a look at the views from the western edge. From here Kinder Reservoir nestles among heathery knolls and green pastures with the plains of Manchester forming a backdrop.

The Pennine Way leads the route down the boulder-scattered north-western nose to Ashop Head, where it meets the ancient Snake Path, linking Hayfield and the Woodlands Valley.

A renovated Pennine Way path continues to Mill Hill, but leave it at the col for a route that turns right on the Snake Path. It crosses peaty terrain before meandering with the banks of the infant

River Ashop. The Boxing Glove Stones' instantly recognisable outline stands out on the soaring cliffs of The Edge.

As the grassland hollow deepens, the path climbs higher up the slopes away from the river and the cliffs sink below the brow of lower hillsides. The path struggles across an area of landslip but soon regains its composure, passing some lonely ruins.

The trees of the Woodlands Valley come into view as the river carves its way through mini-gorges where strata of shale have been exposed. Streams that drain Kinder Plateau break through the grasslands to form cascades. On eerie days when the mist feathers and blurs the moor-tops, the streams seem to tumble out from the sky – plumes of white against the dark heather. Their echoing splashes pierce the murk and the silence of the moor.

The path enters the sprucewoods near Saukin Ridge, but the flirtation is brief. It resumes its course by the chattering river before entering the Woodlands Valley at its meeting with Lady Clough.

Cross the stream using the footbridge that was forsaken earlier in the day and turn left, retracing the outward route northwards through Lady Clough and back to the Birchen Clough car park.

13 Kinder Downfall

Kinder Scout is more often than not climbed from Edale, but it can also be tackled from Hayfield on the western side, where the paths are less eroded. It's the route taken by Benny Rothman and his followers in the famous 1932 Kinder Trespass. Their climb to Kinder Scout was punctuated by threats from gamekeepers and accompanying policemen (see introduction for more detail). Hopefully today's walker finds the situation a bit less eventful.

> **Distance:**
> 8miles/13km
> **Height gain:**
> 1,440ft/440m
> **Walking time:**
> 5 hours
> **Type of walk:**
> A moderate climb to the plateau on easy-to-
> follow paths followed by a walk on the rocky cliff edge then descent on less defined paths across farmland.
> **Start/Finish:**
> Bowden Bridge car park, east of Hayfield. GR048869.

The car park lies in an old quarry where the Kinder Trespassers gathered in an attempt to gain publicity for the freedom to roam the hills of Britain. Nearby Bowden Bridge is an old packhorse bridge.

Go left out of the car park, but this is a pleasant cul-de-sac, winding through the trees and by the banks of the River Kinder. After 500yds/m, leave the lane

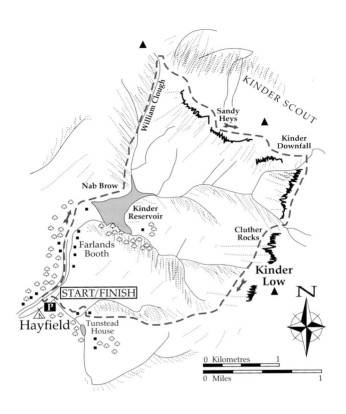

at the footpath signpost and cross a bridge to the east bank of the Kinder, little more than a babbling brook hereabouts. The little path traces the riverside before turning left to rejoin the road just short of the treatment plant buildings.

Another gate bars the way to the grass-covered

dam of Kinder Reservoir, but a cobbled bridleway climbs to the left of the buildings. By now the bouldered flanks of Kinder Scout's western edge rear up above the reservoir shores and the surrounding pastures. As the bridleway draws level with the top of the dam, double-back left, tracing a wall to the top of the field, then turn right to follow a path along the edge of the moor.

Kinder Scout is now in full view, as is Mill Hill, a more rounded knoll known to Pennine Wayfarers as a wet, grassy ridge leading to the even wetter Featherbed Moss. That's for another day.

This route aims for Ashop Head, the col between the two hills, but first it makes a gradual descent into William Clough, where it is joined by a path from the reservoir. The stream is playful here and the path joins the games by flirting with both banks on a regular basis. Heather and moor grass cloak the surrounding hillside as the clough gets narrow and the views more confined. Peat takes a hold on the last stretches to the col and the stream becomes little more than a trickle.

The clough divides. Go left and climb to Ashop Head, where a wide view appears across the empty environs of Black Ashop Moor. Somewhere in that next valley the tourists linger at the Snake Inn, but that's a world apart.

At Ashop Head the Pennine Way is met and the walker sees the problems of erosion that have meant that the moor has had to be inlaid with stone slabs. Some say that they resemble the old causey paths used by ancient travellers, others say they are an intrusion in a wilderness. Whatever your thoughts, you get to keep your feet dry.

Turn right on the slabbed path to the edge and continue on a pleasantly cobbled path climbing and winding through the rocks to gain the plateau. Here the walking gets easy as the path follows the western edge, twisting between the gnarled gritstone rocks.

Below, Kinder Reservoir basks in a landscape of rounded heather hills, squat pale moorland and vast plains that stretch to the skyscrapers of Stockport and Manchester. Farther still, the pallid blue hills of Clwyd and Snowdonia lie along the skyline behind a wispy haze.

The path turns left with the edge and into the cove cut by the infant River Kinder. The tiny Mermaid's Pool rests on a grassy shelf below while a vast jumble of rocks and boulders surround the cleft of Kinder Downfall. More often than not, in summer there is little or no water to produce a waterfall of any stature. In winter, however, the scene can be more spectacular, especially if the wind is from the west, blowing the waterfall back up the hill.

The Kinder cuts a shallow furrow in the plateau's rocks and the path descends to cross it about 100yds/m back from the edge. Those who want to do a little exploration could follow the channel through the peat-hagged top to Kinder Gates, where ramparts of heather and bilberry are studded with huge gritstone outcrops. Otherwise turn right after the river crossing and continue along the edge.

After fording Red Brook, take a right fork (marked in black dashes on the OS Outdoor Leisure Map), leaving the Pennine Way route for a path that heads south-westwards contouring round grassy slopes beneath the rocky edge. There is another fork in the tracks but the routes rejoin above Cluther Rocks to continue the traverse across the steeper flanks of The Three Knolls beneath Kinder Low.

Go through a gate in a fence (GR066867) beneath the grassy spur of Kinder Low End and take the right fork in the paths along the boundary of the moor and farmland. Go over a stile in a wall to the right by some crumbling sheep pens and turn left through a gateway in the nearby field corner. The path descends westwards down a pastured spur, using gates and stiles at the field boundaries. The walled track marked on the map to the east of Tunstead Clough Farm no longer exists and the path across the fields passes to the left of the farmhouse.

Turn right beyond the farmhouse to follow a winding track descending to a metalled lane leading back to the Kinder Reservoir road. Turn left along this to return to the car park.

14 Kinder Scout

Of all the walks to Kinder Scout's edges this one is the most spectacular and, although the most popular, the early riser will find in Edale an idyllic place. The mid-morning crowds are still in their beds or having breakfast. If the sun is out it will be embellishing the castellated crags of Kinder's southern edge with a golden glow and, like a Siren, will be urging the walker to set forth.

Distance:
8 miles/13km
Height gain:
1,675ft/510m
Walking time:
5 hours
Type of walk:
Well-used paths along the valley followed by reasonably firm paths along the rocky edges. Some boulder-hopping on the upper reaches of Grindsbrook Clough.
Start/Finish:
Edale village pay car park. GR124853.

Take the road from the car park into the village, passing beneath the railway, past the attractive spired church to the square by the Nags Head Inn. Follow the tree-lined track opposite the school, heading westwards to the open fields, and continue on a good path beneath the serrated slopes of Grindslow Knoll. The track stays meek and low at this stage, but rewards the traveller with good views down the Edale Valley.

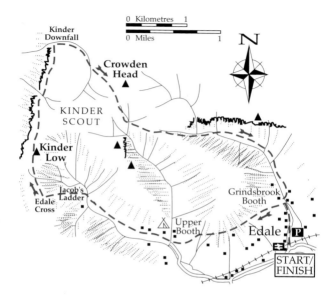

After descending south-west on a good path to the small farming hamlet of Upper Booth, follow a narrow lane leading past Lee End Farm. Follow the unsurfaced lane beyond the farm to an old packhorse bridge that is hemmed in by the steep grassy slopes of Edale Head. The paved Jacob's Ladder path clambers to the ridge at Edale Cross, where the route strikes northwards over grassy moorland.

Mike Harding, in his book Walking the Peak and Pennines, *tells of Jacob the jagger, who would leave his mules to zigzag up the conventional packhorse route while he scrambled to the ridge. His shortcut allowed him time to smoke his pipe before the mules caught up.*

Kinder Scout's rugged southern edge rears up in stark contrast to the gracefully sloping pastures that slink to the valley floor and the angular peaks of Mount Famine and South Head that rise to the west.

After passing beneath the gritstone crags of Swine's Back the route climbs northwards away from the edge and past Edale Rocks to Kinder Low. A concrete trig point squats amid an area where dark peat is liberally sprinkled with gravel and interspersed with boulder.

In the western panorama, Kinder Reservoir nestles in a green pastured hollow, surrounded by heather-clad hills that divide the peak from the plains of Manchester. Tower blocks merge with yet more distant hills on a horizon that fades to Snowdonia, Merseyside and the Irish Sea.

From Kinder Low, trace the path to the western edge where there are views across rock-scattered grassy slopes to the nick of Kinder Downfall. The path descends briefly to ford Red Brook and continues among increasingly rocky scenery to the downfall.

In winter, the popular waterfall can be a spectacular torrent, thundering down on the jumbled rocks below: high winds can blow the waters back on to the plateau. In summer the torrent dries up to become a mere trickle.

The route returns to Edale on the old course of the Pennine Way through Kinder Gates. Follow the crag-lined groove of the infant Kinder as it arcs south-east. At Kinder Gates, huge weather-beaten outcrops jut out from beds of bilberry and heather. The groove shallows and disappears in a maze of peat groughs. Use the firmer beds of the groughs wherever possible to head south-east.

This course should lead to the path along the southern edge in the region of Crowden Tower, a huge gritstone crag overlooking Edale. Here the walker is confronted by a huge rocky ravine, down which Crowden Brook rushes and tumbles before reaching the serenity of the pastured valley.

The path circumvents the top of the ravine, dropping briefly to cross the brook before climbing out across the northern shoulder of Grindslow Knoll. Ignore the right fork, which heads for Grindslow, but continue eastwards to a large cairn marking the start of a bouldery descent down Grindsbrook Clough.

Initially, the going is rough and over bouldery terrain, but a path develops on the northern banks of the brook, which now cascades through its scything ravine in a series of little waterfalls and cataracts.

On further descent the path develops into a wide track and the landscape becomes less severe. Trees and grass clothe the ravine, and heather splashes colour on the hill slopes. Looking backwards, the jagged rocky walls close in to remind the walker of Kinder's austerity. Some gritstone paving slabs lead the walker on to the fields of Edale and a little footbridge allows the crossing of the brook back into the village.

15 Ringing Roger Grindslow Knoll

Ringing Roger and Grindslow Knoll look down on Edale, standing like sentries by the gates of Grindsbrook Clough. Both are fine rock-crested peaks in their own right, but they can be combined in a circular route that also takes in the less frequently visited Crookstone Hill. Before striking for the high ground the route contours Edale in the footsteps of jaggers and climbs to an important crossroads where Roman legions would have marched.

Distance:
9½miles/16km
Height gain:
1,610ft/490m
Walking time:
5/6 hours
Type of walk:
This moderate walk begins as an easy paced route across the fields of Edale. It then climbs to the plateau where it follows narrow paths through bilberry and heather, widening to the well-trodden routes above Grindsbrook. The outing takes on a more serious nature in wintry conditions.
Start/Finish:
Car park, Edale. GR124853.
Note:
The walking is over a permitted access area, which can be closed on shooting days between August 12 and December 10 and also at times of high fire risk.

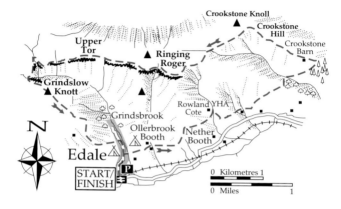

Turn right out of the car park, heading northwards under the railway bridge and past the Rambler Inn, then right again past the National Park Information Centre. A sunken walled track now leads in the shade of some trees, crossing Grinds Brook on a little stone bridge, before heading eastwards across fields.

Edale, the valley, looks at its best. The graceful contours of its verdant lower slopes are accentuated by the patterns of hedgerow and copse, while that great southern ridge of Lose Hill and Mam Tor soars to the skies. To the north, the scene is balanced by the serrated sandy crags of Ringing Roger and Nether Tor. Surrounded by so much beauty the River Noe seems unimpressed as it rustles through the landscape, its chattering drowned only for brief moments by the rumblings of a tractor or hurrying trains.

The cart track continues eastwards to the farming

hamlet of Ollerbrook Booth, which means the livestock enclosure of Alder Brook. Go straight through the farmyard and follow a stony lane eastwards past Nether Ollerbrook towards Cotefield Farm. Take the path passing to the south of the latter, through a couple of gates and a stile.

An easily-missed sign (Footpath to open country), just past the gate and to the left, is where the path divides. The one to be followed leaves the track, climbing left by a hedge. Another footpath signpost points the way as the path swings right, above the woods behind Woodhouse Farm.

The path threads through gorse, bracken and hawthorn trees at the foot of the moor, then transforms into a smooth grassy path that leads into the car park of Edale Youth Hostel at Rowland Cote. Pass immediately in front of the hostel, which is pleasantly situated among mixed woodland, and descend some steps to cross a footbridge over Lady Brook Clough. The path now climbs the opposite banks to contour round a bracken-cloaked moorland spur back into the main valley. A steep climb by a drystone wall on grassy slopes precedes another stream crossing above Clough Farm. A half-mile further east, the path, now a wide engineered track, descends to ford the stream in the partially wooded Jaggers Clough, before climbing once more to high pasture on a hill separating Edale from Woodlands Valley.

The view southwards has widened and includes limestone hills beyond Edale and the belching chimneys of the Hope cement works.

On reaching the five-way junction of tracks at the ridge turn left along what was once a Roman road linking the forts of Melandra at Glossop and Navio near Bradwell. The ancient road climbs to a gate at GR158879. Just beyond it a worn track climbs west across the grassy slopes of Crookstone Hill. Sparse, wind-warped trees decorate the stark terrain, while equally sparse crags fringe the hilltops.

A signpost by a tree in the middle of the moor points the way to a stile in the intake wall. The path climbs towards the hilltop, veering left along the upper slopes, which are now cloaked with thick bilberry and heather. It threads through the crags to join the path along Kinder's southern edge.

The word edge is probably a bit of an exaggeration in the initial stages, for the rocks are sparse and, although steep, the slopes are rounded. The walking is easy, however, and the views dominated by the pointed Win Hill, and the Lose Hill-Mam Tor ridge, which rises from Edale like a colossal hump-backed sea monster.

The little path fords Jaggers Clough and rounds Rowland Cote Moor, where the edge becomes more defined. Beyond the fords at the head of Ollerbrook Clough (in summer they may be dry), detour from the path across a barren area of powdered gritstone and boulder to the prominent rocky arete of Ringing Roger (the echoing rocks).

The rocks offer a fine vantage, overlooking vast heather slopes that plummet into the wide clough of Grindsbrook. Edale's village is in full view, dwarfed by the scale of its surroundings and framed by a mosaic of crazy field patterns.

Returning to the edge path, turn left, following it across Golden Clough to the weatherbeaten outcrops of Nether Tor. In the last part of the 19th century, stone was quarried here to build Edale's parish church.

Below, the chasm of Grindsbrook Clough gouges into Kinder's plateau, with the sentinels of Grindslow Knoll and Upper Tor looking down on the splashing watercourse.

Beyond Nether Tor is Upper Tor, and beyond that the little path detours round the rocky eastern ravine of upper Grinds Brook. At a large cairn the path is joined by the former Pennine Way (Grindsbrook route), which is a quick way down. A better route heads south-east for Grindslow Knoll. The path, which traces the southern rim of Grindsbrook Clough, just misses the summit, and a detour has to be made to see its wide-ranging views down the length of Edale. An eroded path takes a dive down Grindslow's south-east slopes, but for the mountain's sake let it rest and head south instead, to join the path at the foot of the outcrops (GR109866). Take the left fork and a left fork again just short of a wall corner. The path now follows the wall down to join the previously mentioned track at GR113866.

The rutted track descends to a stile in the intake wall. Here a waymarked concessionary path traverses fields and follows a fence. It meets the current Pennine Way (Jacob's Ladder path) at the top of Peat Lane, which leads the route into the village. A right turn will bring the route back past the information centre and the Rambler Inn to the car park.

16 Mill Hill and The Knott

Many walkers know Mill Hill from their journey along the Pennine Way, where it is the anticlimax after the rocky cliffs of Kinder. This walk, however, climbs the quiet way over pleasing heather moors to the summit, where ancient travellers once warily trod on their way across the dark Pennines. The way back is for modern pilgrims who do not mind roughing it amongst deep trackless heather. They will set foot on The Knott, one of those fascinating, rocky tors spied and admired, but rarely visited.

Distance:
4½miles/8km.
Height gain:
920 ft/280m.
Walking time:
2/3 hours.
Type of walk:
Moorland with rough walking across trackless deep heather in the latter stages. Proper walking boots are an essential.
Start/Finish:
Car park, Monks Road, Hollingworth Head, near The Grouse

Inn. GR033903.
Note:
The walk is over a permitted access area, which can be closed on shooting days between August 12 and December 10 and also at times of high fire risk. Conservationists would also argue that the pathless route over The Knott should not be used in the grouse nesting periods between March and May.

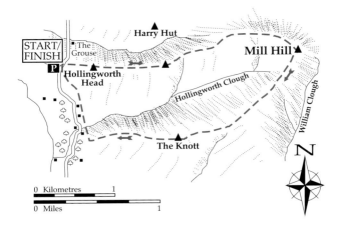

At Hollingworth Head the walker starts high. From
the car park go a short way east down Monks Road
back to the main Glossop-Hayfield road. Immediately across it, beyond the roadside stile, a
Landrover track climbs a grassy hillside, flecked
with a little heather and bilberry. To the north,
beyond a little wooded clough, a heather hill
marked on the maps as Harry Hut, has a rocky top.

Beyond a gate and stile the track becomes a deep
peaty groove in thick heather. To the south The
Knott bobbles in and out of view with each
undulation of the terrain, like a curious dark whale
in the ocean.

*On reaching the summit of Burnt Hill, Kinder Scout comes
into view, peaking out from above the grassy south-west
arm of Mill Hill. Mill Hill itself stretches to the horizon,*

becoming more grassy and moss-like each step of the way.

The path to it becomes wetter on gaining height, a feature that Pennine Wayfarers will remember well. Fortunately there always seems to be a way round those wet bits.

The ruins of an old United States Liberator warplane still lie scattered across a peaty channel high on Mill Hill's slopes.

A stake lodged in a pile of stones marks the top of the hill. To the north the land drops away to a moorland col at the head of the wild Ashop valley. Kinder Scout's squarish massif, fringed with gritstone, rises from its moorland plinth with barren slopes of moor grass, reeds and a little heather. Recently-placed paving slabs form a stone highway across the reddish-hued and very wet ridge between Mill Hill, Moss Castle and Featherbed Moss.

For the walker who cannot resist the temptation of extending the walk to Kinder Scout it's just a matter of summoning up enough energy, dropping down to the col and climbing the well-defined rock-inlaid path to the plateau. They would descend to Kinder Reservoir dam by the descent route described in the Kinder Downfall walk, before rejoining the main route by way of the bridleway across Middle Moor (from GR054882).

The main route to The Knott is short, mostly trackless, and quite tough. Ignore the track that heads westwards into Hollingworth Clough, but head south-west on the crest of the moorland spur.

It is trackless at first. A slimy channel in the eroded peat helps for a while, but when it veers right towards Hollingworth Clough a vague path/sheep-track continues along the spur with The Knott directly ahead. As the path nears the edge overlooking William Clough and Kinder Reservoir it is joined by another from the left.

By now the heather has increased, but as the heather gets coarser it swallows the path. On the last descent to the col between Mill Hill and The Knott it's just a matter of finding the most comfortable way – the odd sheep track and patch of bare peat makes this possible.

By looking to The Knott the walker will see a wavering dark route to the summit rocks. It turns out to be a very narrow path indeed when reached, but the summit is a good one.

The rocks on the north side offer a good perch overlooking Hollingworth Clough and the wide undulating heathland. A small stony cairn and a luxuriant carpet of bilberry and heather cap the true summit, which is blessed with good views back to Kinder and south to Cracken Edge and Mount Famine.

The descent from the top is also trackless and across more deep heather and bilberry. A few boulders, just big enough and just loose enough to trip the unsuspecting walker, lie concealed in the undergrowth – take care. Keep to the northern edge of the moor for the best ground.

The difficulties end on reaching the bridleway by a

footbridge over the stream. A memorial by the bridge commemorates Thomas Boulger, who worked to preserve footpaths for 40 years until 1963. Over the bridge a heavily-grooved cart track takes the route north by a stone wall at the moor's edge. A path cuts a corner by an old quarry. Rather than coming down to the road early take the right fork in the tracks. This terminates at the roadside stile encountered at the beginning of the walk.

17 Win Hill

Win Hill is one of the finest hills in the Peak, its diminutive summit being crested with good rock and blessed with the region's widest and most fascinating panoramas. This walk, tackling the hill from the south-east, would be particularly well suited to August, when much of the air is sweet with heather.

Distance:
7½ miles/12km
Height gain:
1,050 ft/320m
Walking time:
4/5 hours
Type of walk:
Moderate walk but with steep climbs to Win Hill's summit. A mixture of narrow paths through scrub, forest tracks and well-defined ridge routes.
Start/Finish:
Heatherdene car park/picnic area near Ladybower Dam.
GR203858.

Head south from the car park through the picnic area to the Ladybower dam. A footpath descends beneath the grass covered banks of the dam to the lane at Yorkshire Bridge.

From the roadside just south of the bridge, a narrow and overgrown path climbs through tangled but not unattractive scrub consisting of tall bracken, bramble, wild rose, and hawthorn with a splash of purple and pink added by thistles and willowherb. The path meets the trackbed of an old railway that

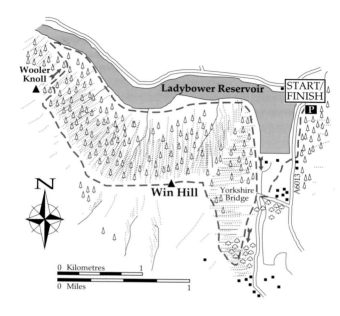

linked Bamford and Fairholmes. It was built to supply material to the Derwent and Howden reservoirs, but reopened for constructing Ladybower.

The climb continues on the narrow, winding path, which is staggered slightly to the left at the other side of the old railway line. The thick scrub relents and the path crosses fields scattered with twisted hawthorn trees. The path is faint in the initial stages, but any doubts about it are allayed by the positioning of stone gateposts and adjacent squeeze stiles. The farm that once stood hereabouts was deserted for the building of the reservoir.

By now views across the Derwent Valley to Bamford Rocks and Higger Tor have added a little spice to the walk. Looking back the heather-clad, rocky tors of Derwent Edge arc away from the shores of Ladybower.

After twisting through more scrub the path reaches the top of Thornhill Carrs. Ignore the stile in the hedge (the path down to Hope), but double-back (right) on a better-defined track that climbs north-west up the spur towards Win Hill. It soon becomes a delightful sunken track. I saw it in August: the bright yellow of the gorse and the pink of the tightly-interlocking heather made a stunning foreground to the wide views that included the long eastern edges between Stanage and Baslow.

Keep with the main track (left fork) at its junction with a narrow downhill path (GR193846). It enters the Winhill plantations where it meets the direct route to Win Hill. Turn left and climb the wide and eroded path through the heather. Beyond a fence and stile lies the summit, almost bald of vegetation but endowed with a jagged crest of rock.

In August, the surroundings are completely pink with heather. The ridge falls away to reveal the contrasting emerald pastures of Edale, the pyramidal Lose Hill and the great ridge to Mam Tor. To the north, more heather, this time clothing the flanks of Kinder Scout. Add Ladybower Reservoir and the edges of Stanage and Derwent and it all goes to make up a striking summit panorama.

The path scrambles down the western rocks and traces the heathery spine of the north-west ridge. This is one of the finest stretches of the walk – easy after the stiff climb, but still offering wide views.

As the heather ceases, the path is joined by a bridleway from Aston, then comes to a crossroads near the forest's edge on Wooler Knoll. Turn right here to follow a sunken grassy track into the forest. The track bends left, then right before coming to a T-junction with a forestry road. Turn left along it down to a wider stony forest road along the shores of Ladybower Reservoir. Turn right to follow the new track along the shores.

The crusty twin knolls of Crook Hill capture centre-stage across the lake, but they disappear from view as the road rounds the headland to the huge Ladybower Dam.

Continue along a stony walled lane to the road at Yorkshire Bridge, turn left along it for a short way, then follow the outward route beneath the dam and back to the car park at Heatherdene.

18 Lose Hill and the Roman Road

This walk is one for your conscience. The wondrous beauty of the route along the Great Ridge from Mam Tor to Lose Hill has to be weighed up against the erosion that has been caused by its over-use — mainly by the footsteps of the masses who start from the high Mam Tor car parks. The highlights are the cliffs of Back Tor, and the views from the eastern outpost, Lose Hill.

Distance: 9 miles/15km	**Type of walk:** A moderate to strenuous walk with many undulations.
Height gain: 1,380ft/420m	
Walking time: 5/6 hours	**Start/Finish:** Car park, Edale. GR124853.

Once out of the car park follow the road, right towards Barber Booth before turning left on the gated lane past Hardenclough Farm. The lane climbs further, becoming sunken and shaded by trees on the winding approach to Greenlands. Turn left at this second farm over a stile by a gate. A stony footpath heads east through new woodland before climbing the hillsides to Hollins Cross.

Arriving at Hollins Cross the walker sees a monument to rambler Tom Hyett, surrounded by the effects of erosion and the popularity of the

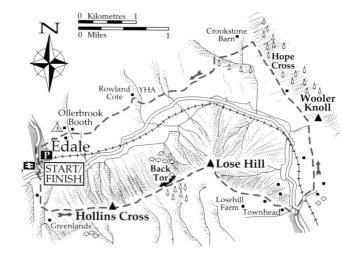

ridge route. Turn left here to climb a subsidiary summit before tackling Back Tor. A landslip has exposed the rock strata here, and a line of gaunt and weather-beaten pines gives the peak a Mohican haircut. The path to the summit is steep and eroded but the pull short-lived. It's now an easy ridge-walk to Lose Hill. This grassy pyramid offers unparalleled views of Edale, the Hope Valley, Win Hill and the cliffs of Stanage Edge.

Descend south from Lose Hill to a stile on a path inlaid with stone cobbles. From here the path veers south-east down to a further stile in a fence, before joining a path from Lose Hill Farm amongst an area patched with bracken. The route now follows a line of trees past the barn, Lose Hill End, to exit at a laneside stile opposite Townhead Farm.

Turn left down the lane, then right at the junction to descend to the Edale road at Townhead Bridge. Those in need of refreshment could detour south to the Cheshire Cheese pub; otherwise turn left past some cottages and a derelict barn to the tree-enshrouded bridge.

A walled lane on the far side of the bridge takes the walk beneath the railway. By Fulwood Stile Farm the lane turns left to climb the pastured hillside. Beyond a gate at the edge of open country the route joins an old highway once used by Roman soldiers. It rakes up the hillside to the ridgetop at Hope Cross (GR162874 – marked as Guide Post on the OS Outdoor Leisure Map).

The Hope Cross stone is medieval: the 1737 refers to the date of engraving. There was once a chapel nearby, where a traveller could seek refuge and be fed, not only with the words of God but with worldly sustenance.

Conifer plantations of the Woodlands Valley come right to the top of the ridge hereabouts and form a backdrop to the cross. The old highway continues by them to reach an intersection of five tracks.

Looking east, the forests of the Woodlands and Derwent Valleys surround the sinuous tentacles of Ladybower Reservoir. To the north and west slopes of heather and bracken rise to the Kinder plateau.

Turn left on the wide track that gradually descends

to ford Jaggers Clough. The track continues beyond a gate in a high stone wall and climbs out of the clough past the regenerated Backside Wood. The renovated track doubles back up the hillside to the top of the woods and traverses pastureland on the shoulder of the hillside.

As the track descends to Clough Farm abandon it for a path that climbs by the intake wall above the farm. The path then descends steep grassy banks to cross a stream, and climbs once more past some woods before rounding a bracken-clad spur into the deep-set clough of Lady Booth Brook. Here it declines gradually to woodlands surrounding the Edale youth hostel, Rowland Cote.

Cross the little footbridge over the brook and climb some steps. This brings the path to the hostel. Pass in front of it and go through the car park to follow a grassy permissive path that skirts the lower moor. After passing through an area of gorse and hawthorn above some woods, the path curves left by a footpath signpost to descend alongside a hedge at the far end of a field.

At the bottom of the field turn right along a well-defined track linking the farming hamlets of Nether Booth below and Ollerbrook Booth to the west. Beyond Cotefield Farm the track becomes a stony lane terminating in the farmyard of Ollerbrook Booth.

Unless a drink at the Nags Head is the order of the day, turn half left from the back of Ollerbrook's farmyard on a track traversing more fields. It dips into a shady bower to cross Grinds Brook on a stone bridge and continues as a walled track that meets the road into the village close to the information centre. Turn left along the road passing the Rambler Inn, and under the railway back to the car park.

19 Rushup Edge and Crowden Tower

This splendid circular walk discovers the high hills ringing the head of Edale. First it tackles Rushup Edge, a great grassy ridge with fine views of the limestone White Peak and the gritstone scenery to the north. Rounding Edale on peaty whalebacks it comes upon the weird world of Kinder Scout gritstone, then swoops down to valley booths using the spectacular Crowden Clough path.

Distance:
8½ miles/14km
Height gain:
1,445ft/440m
Walking time:
5 hours
Type of walk:
Good ridge walking on Rushup Edge after a steep climb from the valley. Slightly wetter on Brown Knoll followed by a good edge path on Kinder Scout. The descent to Crowden is steep and

the river crossings could be difficult after periods of heavy rain or snow.
Start/Finish:
Car park Barber Booth. GR107847, by railway viaduct.
Note: The walk crosses a permitted access area, which can be closed on shooting days between August 12 and December 10 and also at times of high fire risk.

The lane from the car park winds under the railway viaduct to Barber Booth, where it meets the road from Rushup Edge. Immediately opposite at the T-junction, a footpath signpost points the

trackless way eastwards across fields bordered with hawthorns.

Views are channelled by the hillslopes on either side. Right, the greenery of Mam Tor counterbalances Kinder Scout's crag-fringed flanks of heather and bracken on the left.

The path dips to cross a tree-enshrouded stream north of Upper Holt Farm. In spring and early summer the wetland surrounds are filled with wild flowers. Continuing eastwards between the farms of Small Clough and Greenhill, the path reaches the woods of Holden Clough. Cross the stile into the woods, then turn immediately right on a footpath tracing the west banks of the stream. Do not confuse this with the parallel metalled access lane to Greenlands Farm.

The route gets steeper as it enters open country, with Mam Tor Nick visible on the skyline. When the path reaches the road, follow it to the first bend, then take the path on the right, which cuts a corner to the Nick. Turn right on the path on to Rushup Edge and climb the right-hand banks to the footpath on the ridge top (the parallel bridleway stays to the south of the ridge, losing the lofty views over Edale).

The eroded footpath climbs to the right of a wall along the grassy ridge. It passes a Bronze Age burial mound near the summit of Lord's Seat.

The whole ridge offers wide views across Edale to crag-fringed Kinder Scout, but on Lord's Seat those views extend westwards across the pasture-crazed valley to the high rounded hills at its head.

The path, still to the right of the ridge wall, descends to a footpath signpost at a junction of paths. Turn right here following the path marked to Barber Booth. As it swings right (a spot marked by a tall post), leave it for a sketchy track heading north-west along a wide peaty whaleback ridge.

It is worth noting at this point that, although most of the ridge is covered by an agreed access area or owned by the National Trust, some of it is on private land with no right of way. Fortunately, the owner does not object to walkers crossing. In the event of the present or some future owner withdrawing this concession, continue down the bridleway to Chapel Gate Track, which descends to meet the longer route at Barber Booth.

The path along the ridge soon develops into a well-worn track climbing to Brown Knoll. The castellated tower to the left is an air shaft for the Gowburn railway tunnel, which conveys the Manchester-Sheffield trains. Beyond Brown Knoll descend to a wall corner, where a path from Chinley Head joins from the left. Here the River Sett has cut a scything grassy hollow shaded by the slopes of Kinderlow End and Mount Famine.

A short way downhill, the path meets the busy bridleway that has climbed out of Edale on Jacob's Ladder on its way to Edale Cross. Cut across it on the Pennine Way route climbing towards the Swine's Back and the prominent Edale Rocks. Leave the Pennine Way for a path forking right along the edge high above the head of the valley. The path passes beneath Edale Rocks, though a quick detour could include them, to reach Noe Stool, a gigantic gritstone perch lying close to the watercourse that shares its name and formed Edale's fertile valley.

In retrospective summer views Swine's Back looks so green compared to the surrounding grey rock and brown peat. Its distinctive shape sets it apart from the brown, rounded hills that lie beyond.Further wanderings along the edge bring the walk to Pym Chair, another throne for giants, and one that was probably named after the 17th-century Member of Parliament, John Pym.

Looking north Kinder plateau rises a few feet higher. Outside summer it's an undulating quagmire of peat: in summer the peat goes flaky and can be a pleasant springy surface on which to detour north-west in search of the pile of stones marking the 636m spot height that is the summit.

Most will opt for the continuation along the edge to the stone soldiers capping the next high spot. The Wool Packs, a spread of weather-smoothed outcrops capping the peat, have been likened to zoo animals and are sometimes referred to as Whipsnade. Wander through them or use them as table and chairs for alfresco dining.

The route now heads for Crowden Tower. The gigantic outcrop, which can be seen for miles across Edale, overlooks a huge rocky ravine down which Crowden Brook rushes and tumbles. This will be the route of descent. The path turns north-east to descend to the place where Crowden Brook tumbles over the edge. Many walkers climb alongside the bouldery watercourse, but as a route of descent it would be awkward. Instead follow a narrow level path traversing higher slopes to the west of the stream. It joins a less interesting short-cut path that has come from Crowden Tower and together they descend very steeply the grassy hillslopes to the banks of the brook.

The path now follows the brook, flirting with both banks. The fords are easy in the summer, but can be tricky after heavy rain. There are several waterfalls en route and many places for a paddle to cool those feet.

Lower down, ash and rowans scatter the banks and the route comes to the edge of open country. A wide track peels off to the left, but the path to be used on this occasion continues south beyond a gate. It crosses a footbridge shaded by tall rowans to change to the west bank. From here it squeezes and undulates through recently planted woodland of pine, larch, birch and oak. Colourful wildflowers, including bluebells, daffodils and primroses proliferate in this delightful spot.

After passing the campsite on the far bank of the brook, the path descends in steps to the road at Upper Booth. Turn left along the road and left again into the farmyard. Turn right and follow the path marked to Barber Booth. The path, sketchy at first, but well waymarked with yellow arrows, heads south-east across fields with Mam Tor directly ahead. On entering another campsite, it joins a track leading to the railway, near Whitmore Lea Farm.

Leave the track at the viaduct to the west of the farm to cross the footbridge over the River Noe and go through the trees to the road just east of the car park.

The Western Outliers

The western hills of the Peak District mingle with industrial Manchester and the plains of Cheshire and Staffordshire. To call them a range would be a misnomer for, with the exception of the Shining Tor group, they are a collection of small peaks surrounded by a network of little valleys.

They have something else in common – gritstone. Most have a good shape, perhaps more so than their loftier neighbours of the heartlands. Shuttlingsloe has been called the Cheshire Matterhorn, though the Cheshire Ingleborough would be more fitting. Lantern Pike and South Head above Chinley have distinctive outlines that make them recognisable for many a mile. Both look across to Kinder Scout and Bleaklow and offer short walks for short winter days or long summer evenings.

Cown and Cracken Edges on the industrial side of the Peak were once heavily quarried, but silence has returned to the moors and the harsh rockfaces are slowly being eroded to merge with their surroundings. Both hills offer great views as does the whole of Shining Tor Ridge, whose crags rarely surface through the heather and grasses until Windgather Rocks to the north.

Pride of place has to go to Hen Cloud and The Roaches, those last bastions of the North, which frown on the Midlands like statues of warlords in great city squares.

20 Coombes Rocks & Cown Edge Rocks

Coombes Rocks lie on the north-western extremities of the Peak District National Park. The partially-quarried iron-stained cliffs look down on the village of Charlesworth and its surrounding pastureland in the Etherow Valley. On the other side of the hill, the confusingly named Cown Edge Rocks look more natural, if less spectacular. They offer a much more rural outlook, facing Bleaklow and Kinder Scout. This short circular walk from Charlesworth allows an exploration of both sets of rocks and the chance to see more celebrated peaks from a different angle.

Distance:
4 miles/6km
Height gain:
1,082ft/330m
Walking time:
2 hours
Type of walk:
Short walk but with steady climbs. Stream crossings in Close Wood could be tricky

when in spate (see alternative in such circumstances)
Start/Finish:
Charlesworth. Roadside parking on the Simmondley road near the school. GR007929 – be considerate.

Turn right just past the school and climb on the metalled Back Lane. Take the left fork by some cottages (GR007927). The stony track veers right, climbing to the northern edge of the coomb above

Close Wood. A stile to the right gives access to a footpath tracing the edge known as The Banks. On reaching the flinted track to Coombes Farm (GR014925), turn left for a few yards then right at a stile by some sheep pens. A grassy path continues the climb round Coombes Edge, passing close to some conifer plantations to the top of the rocks.

Looking west across the vast landslip known as Mares Back and the farm pastures and woodland beyond, the distant tower blocks of Stockport lead the eye still further into the hazy environs of Greater Manchester and the pale South Pennine hills.

Cross the stile to the left by a strip plantation of spruce (GR018918) and follow a grooved track in the grassy ridge beyond. It leads south-west, parallel to the sprucewoods. On reaching a dip in the ridge, turn left to view a second series of rocks.

The Cown Edge Rocks may be more sparse, but they are more natural and more rewarding to the eye. From them the walker looks across Rocks Farm and its mellow valley pastures to the hills – Bleaklow, Mill Hill and Kinder Scout.

Return to the track and cross a stile to the left, continuing south-west along the airy ridge. On meeting another track that has climbed from the road at Plainsteads Farm, turn right following it west for a short way to a sharp left-hand bend (GR013911). A stile on the right marks the start of a right of way (pathless) that descends north-west on a grassy spur that forms the southern arm around Far Coombes. It meets a sunken grassy track, which zigzags down to Far Coombes Farm.

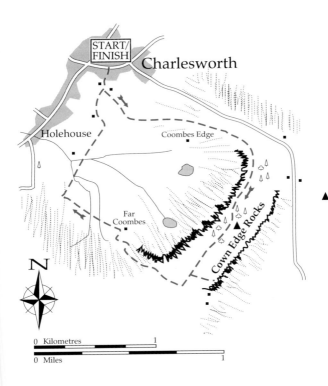

Ignore the little stile in the fence halfway down the zigzags: it is the start of the path beneath the cliffs to Coombes Farm.

At Far Coombes Farm turn left alongside a new stone wall to the gravel-surfaced access track. Follow this past a newly-built and substantial stone house (not on the 1995 map) and some outbuildings.

Just beyond them on the right (GR004917) is a stile. In winter or after rainfall the next stage of the route beyond this stile could be tricky, for a couple of streams that need to be forded could be in spate. In this case, continue down the access track to the road at Bot Wood, then follow it back to Charlesworth. Otherwise, cross the stile and head north-north-east on an overgrown grassy path. Beyond a second stile in a wooden fence, the path descends along the left edge of a field into woodland. Now muddy, the path fords a brook, before climbing north out of the woodland to a rickety gate near an old mill (GR005922), which is now used as a factory.

At the entrance to the factory turn right to cross a stile and follow the southern edge of the mill pond. Another stile on the left allows entry into Close Wood, where the path descends to cross another stream before climbing to the fields to the north.

Another new house (GR007923 and not on the 1995 map) complicates route finding. The path goes to the right of it to reach Boggart Lane, a stony track that passes Close Farm before climbing to the outward route by the cottages at the end of Back Lane. From here steps should be retraced down the lane to the start.

21 Cracken Edge and South Head

Rising between the Goyt and Sett valleys, a shapely hill, Chinley Churn, promises much to the walker. Its summit, unfortunately, is out of bounds and has been tamed by farming. As a result it wears the green mantle of pasture and is imprisoned by stone walls. The quarryman, however, has abandoned his claims on the hill and left a legacy of boulder and rock, and a network of tracks that saunter along the high eastern cliffs known as Cracken Edge. This short walk combines the edge with South Head, an equally shapely peak by the side of Kinder Scout.

Distance:	paths, quarry and farm
5 miles/8km	tracks and a little
Height gain:	moorland.
950ft/290m	**Start/Finish:**
Walking time:	Chinley War
3 hours	Memorial, Maynestone
Type of walk:	Road. G041827.
Moderate walk on field	Roadside car parking.

From the war memorial follow Maynestone Road north-eastwards, but abandon it for a signposted path (GR042828) through a narrow ginnel on the left. Beyond a step-stile the path climbs across fields towards the quarried cliffs of Cracken Edge.

The path veers a little to the left to climb gorse-clad

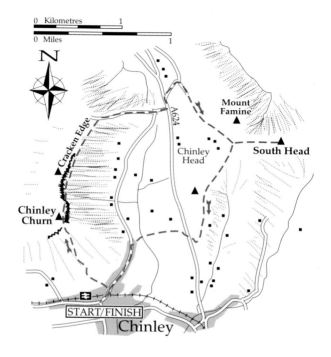

scrubby slopes to reach a cart track. Turn right
along this, then left shortly after on a path passing
between two farmhouses. It goes through a gate
past the farm on the right before climbing to the
lower edge of the quarries.

*In views to the north-east, Kinder Scout's rocky edges jut
out from behind the grassy peaks of Mount Famine and
South Head. South, the rumbles from heavy lorries and*

railway trains turn walkers' heads towards Chinley and its larger neighbour, Chapel-en-le-Frith.

Initially the route above the farm fields is a bit sketchy. Veer right past a large hawthorn tree at the base of the grassy banks to pick up a quarry track that zigzags up the slopes before heading north beneath rust-coloured quarry cliffs. Cross the simple stile in a fence that bisects the track, then climb by the fence to the top wall above the cliffs. To the west, high cultivated pastures rise to the summit trig point of Chinley Churn. More interestingly, Kinder Scout is now in full view, stretching across the skyline, with the gorge of the Kinder Downfall waterfall and the curious Swine's Back Knoll capturing attention.

Turn right to follow a sheep track along the edge for a short while, then cut right on a grassy ramp between two quarried hollows to descend to a prominent grassy track that runs beneath the top edge and above some thin woodland consisting largely of hawthorn.

The views now have improved, and unsightly quarry scars have been subdued by new vegetation. The slopes below plummet to Otter Brook, which wriggles amid pastures on its course from Chinley Head.

The path declines past the old cottage of Whiterakes, which sadly looks as if it has been recently abandoned, before meeting a walled cart track from Hillheads Farm. Turn right on the track and descend to a metalled lane by a house known as Peep-o-Day. Facing eastwards as it does, the house catches the first rays of sunshine from over the hills.

Continue down the lane for a few yards and turn left down the busy A624 (thankfully there is a pavement). Cross the road after 150yds/m to climb on an old cart track past the crater of an old quarry before turning right at a T-junction. The new track climbs south-south-east across the lower grassy slopes of Mount Famine before curving round to a pass beneath South Head, a huge, grassy dome overlooking the upper Sett Valley. The track contours round the northern side of the peak, but an obvious route leaves it to climb to the summit.

Kinder's western edge has all but disappeared behind Kinderlow End's grassy spur, but the scything Sett Valley and the pretty field patterns surrounding South End farm are perfectly framed by the craggy rim of Mount Famine and the woods of Hayfield's Kinder Bank. In the opposite direction the day's earlier wanderings on Cracken Edge can be plotted with ease.

Retrace the route back to the track at the col and go through the gate by the more easterly of the access notices (GR056846). Just beyond the gate in the left wall, a pole marks a skilfully-concealed stile, which should be crossed before descending south-westwards to a walled grassy track. This leads to a crossroads of routes north of Andrews Farm. Go straight on into what, in winter, can be a very muddy field. The path soon develops into a track and joins the cart track from Andrews Farm.

On reaching Hayfield Road (A624) turn right for

50yds/m then cross to the signposted footpath across the fields (GR051835). The path cuts diagonally to the right corner of the first field (north-west) before following a wall down towards Otter Brook. As an old field boundary comes in from the right the path turns half left to cross the brook on a little stone-slabbed bridge.

A muddy path now climbs out through scrubby woodland to a minor road (Maynestone Road). Turn left and follow it back to the start.

22 Lantern Pike

Lantern Pike, like many of the Peak's western outliers, offers pleasant short walks with wide views of loftier surrounding hills. The walking, like the landscape, is gentle compared with Kinder and Bleaklow. This circular route, based on Hayfield and the Sett Valley, takes full advantage using a combination of cart tracks, leafy lanes and a ridge path to the superb little summit.

Distance:
4¹/₂miles/7km
Height gain:
560 ft/170m
Walking time:
2/3 hours
Type of walk:
An easy walk on the trackbed of an old railway, lanes and tracks with a short climb to a little moorland summit.
Start/Finish:
Pay car park at the Hayfield end of the Sett Valley Trail.
GR036869.

The first part of the route to little Lantern Pike follows the Sett Valley Trail, on the trackbed of a railway that until 1970 linked Manchester and New Mills with Hayfield.

The old track leads west from the back of the car park through an avenue of trees and shrubs. Glimpses of Lantern Pike appear through the trees and across the river, its steep pastured slopes rising to a shapely dome, fringed with sparse crags.

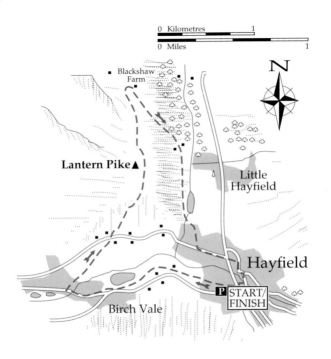

Nature walks lead off the track, but ignore these and stay with the track until the road crossing at Birch Vale, where a right turn along the road passes a factory and some terraced cottages. Just beyond the latter, climb right on a cobbled track (GR020869) past a weaver's whitewashed cottage and into the shade of more trees.

Beyond a gate, the track meets a metalled farm lane at a hairpin bend. Follow its upper course north-west to a country road (GR024874). Staggered to the right across the road, a tarred bridleway ascends further beneath the slopes of Sunny Side. Beyond the last cottage it degenerates into an unsurfaced track emerging on the high, open fellsides, which are cloaked with gorse, bilberry and heather. Ignore the track descending right to Upper Cliffe Farm, but follow the left fork beyond the next gate, which is highlighted by a National Trust sign.

Turn left here and follow a grassy wallside path climbing over heather slopes to the ridge, where it is just a short stroll to Lantern Pike's summit.

Lantern Pike was donated to the National Trust in 1950, following its purchase by subscription as a memorial to Edwin Royce, who fought for the freedom to roam these hills. A summit view indicator, which also commemorates the life of Royce, records the 360 degree panoramas.

To the east the walker looks across to the craggy diadem on the heather-clad Knott, and onwards to the cliffs of Kinder Scout where the Kinder Downfall's rushing waters will be spectacular if in spate. Much of Bleaklow hides behind Mill Hill's extensive moors, but in views to the south, beyond Cracken Edge and the shapely Mount Famine, the rounded ridges above the Goyt Valley rise to Shining Tor.

A path continues north from Lantern Pike, descending slopes flecked with cotton grass. Beyond another gate at the northern boundary of the National Trust estate, the path meets the track abandoned earlier. Follow this across grassy moor to a five-way footpath signpost just to the west of Blackshaw Farm.

Double back to follow a wall south-east. Do not confuse this with the better defined track that heads south. A good path develops. Beyond a little stile it descends beneath the eastern fringe of the moor, passing the top edge of Hey Wood. Here impressive pines, oaks and beech grow healthy and tall. The woods thin out to be replaced by hawthorns, and the mill at Little Hayfield appears in the valley bottom. The path joins the access track of pretty Cliffbank Farm. Where the access track doubles back down the hillside, leave it for a path heading south. The sounds of water tumbling down weirs filter through the woodland to the left.

As the footpath divides, take the left fork, a narrow path descending to a cluster of cottages, where a lane takes over, descending to the minor road (GR033873) on the outskirts of Hayfield.

Turn left along the road, past the school, then, just before the A624 flyover, turn half right on a path through a little park to the riverbank of the Sett. Follow the riverbank beneath the road bridge and into Hayfield centre at Market Street.

The centre of Hayfield is quite attractive and can offer a choice of cafes, shops and inns to serve the walker well-earned refreshment. To get back to the car park, turn right down Fisher Bridge and cross the busy A624 with care to the New Mills road.

23 Shining Tor and the Goyt Valley

Shining Tor crowns a long ridge of heather and peat overlooking the popular Goyt valley on one side and the plains of Cheshire on the other. This circular walk contrasts the austere landscapes of the high places with the park-like gardens of Errwood. Always there is wildlife, whether it be the plovers or curlews of the moor or herons and mallards on the lakes. If you want to add colour to your walk go in late May or early June when the rhododendrons of Errwood will be in bloom.

Distance:
11 miles/18 km
Height gain:
1,705ft/520m
Time taken:
7 hours
Type of walk:
Varied mix of peaty moorland and woodland paths, lanes, and the park-like paths of the Erwood Estate.
Start/Finish:
Roadside car park on the A5002, 1 mile south of Whaley Bridge. GR009799.
Map: OS Outdoor Leisure 24 White Peak.

Taxal's square-towered church peeps through the trees from its perch across the Goyt Valley, and an approach to it follows on a zigzag gravel path that descends to cross the lively river using a footbridge which spans two large stone-built parapets remaining from a previous construction.

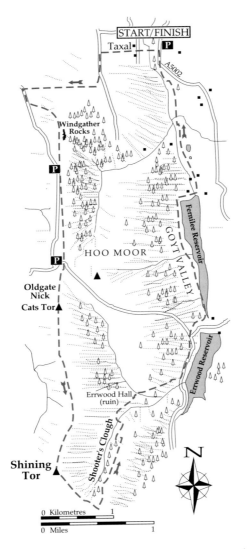

START/FINISH

Taxal P

A5002

Windgather
Rocks

P

GOYT VALLEY

Fernilee Reservoir

HOO MOOR

P

Oldgate
Nick
Cats Tor

Errwood Reservoir

Errwood Hall
(ruin)

Shooter's Clough

Shining
Tor

N

0 Kilometres 1

0 Miles 1

125

Once across the bridge a stony path climbs out of the valley, passing between the church and its graveyard. A cluster of chocolate-box cottages surround the church in a hamlet that has been allowed to keep its serenity while the world passes by on the A-road. Turn left on meeting the metalled lane, then right on a footpath signposted to Taxal Edge. Guided by a stone wall to the right for most of the way, it climbs west across fields with primitive stiles allowing progress over the cross walls.

Turn left along the high lane shaded by some pine woods and the brow of Taxal Moor. At the southern tip of the woods climb on the grassy track raking south-west up the moor. It cuts through terrain studded with larch and rhododendron, heather and bilberry and later swings west to the ridge.

Kettleshulme's scattered cottages bask in a pastured valley hiding from the elements in the shadow of Sponds Hill.

Unfortunately there are no direct rights of way from here along the ridge to Taxal Edge, so once over the stile, descend westwards, veering slightly away from the drystone wall to the left. At the far end of the field, a stile by a five-bar gate gives access to a country lane opposite Wright's Farm.

Turn left along the lane for a short way, but abandon it for a signposted path on the left climbing diagonally across fields back towards the ridge. The path turns southwards just short of a farm and crosses several stiles to reach a cart track at GR996788. Turn left along it, passing a cottage adjacent to the farm. Just past the cottage turn right through a gateway and climb south by a wall along the pastured ridge to Windgather Rocks.

More often than not climbers will be practising on the squat crags of millstone grit, for these are popular with beginners who tackle them from the nearby car park.

Beyond Windgather Rocks, the path runs parallel to the lane but the two are separated by a stone wall so the walker is left in peace. The pastoral scenes give way to wild moorland, shaded at first by the pines of the Goyt Forest. As the path veers half left and away from the road it enters a more sombre scene, where dark walls crumble into the rushes and heather.

The tarred lane at Pym Chair follows the course of the Street, a Roman road that straddled the Goyt Valley on its way to Buxton. The continuing path along the ridge is staggered to the right. Here peat takes hold and the going is a little harder.

Small crags litter the western slopes of Oldgate Nick and Cats Tor, but a little hill on the horizon captures the attention, rising like a pyramid from distant valleys. Shutlingsloe is a Siren, tantalising the walker, who would surely trade his squelchy ridge route for the one to its bold peak.

As Cats Tor is surmounted, Shining Tor appears, a sizeable angular escarpment with its own moorland coombe. Parts of the path to it have been resurfaced with gravel and chippings, others are squelchier than ever. Aspects improve from the summit trig point, where extensive panoramas encompass

Shutlingsloe, the Macclesfield Forest and The Roachesto the south, while the mottled undulating mosses of Goyt and Axe Edge sprawl to the east.

A gravel path, signposted 'To the Cat and Fiddle', cuts south-east across the moors to the saddle at the head of Shooter's Clough. Here it climbs to cross a stile in the wall at GR001732. Refreshments at the Cat and Fiddle are a little under a mile away down the track to the right. If they are not required, continue left on a sunken grassy track descending a spur separating Shooter's Clough and the Goyt Valley.

The map promises good views, but to the left a tall drystone wall imprisons the eyes, leaving them to dwell on mossy hillsides that decline to Errwood Reservoir where sailing dinghies often scud across the waters.

Reality offers something the map only hints at, however, and there is a break in the wall. A signpost promises a route to Errwood Hall and a delightful grassy path fulfils that promise, zig-zagging the steep slopes, which are clad with bilberry, heather and rhododendron.

Oak and pine line the path, while down in the valley bottom there are impressive mature larches and firs. More of those rhododendrons dab extra colour to the heather moors rising beyond them.

Built for the Grimshawe family in 1830, Errwood Hall and its estate would have stood amid a much wilder scene than today. The wildness was diminished by the building of the reservoirs (Fernilee 1938, and Errwood 1967), the widespread planting of coniferous woodland in the 1960s, and the influx of the motoring tourists.

The path fords the stream at the bottom of the clough. It then follows its west banks, cutting through thick bushes of rhododendron before surfacing in fields close to Errwood Hall's forest-clad knoll. Turn right at some old enclosures to follow a cart track round the southern flanks of the knoll to Erwood Hall, where only some arches and the foundations remain. The hall had to be demolished for the construction of the reservoir in the mid 1930s.

Beyond the hall the track continues round the north side of the knoll fording a stream at GR006748 before doubling back through the pine woods to the shores of Errwood Reservoir at Shooter's Clough Bridge.

Follow the road to the dam and descend on a narrow path through the woods. It meets a wide stony track that follows the western shores of Fernilee Reservoir. Ignore the paths climbing to the left, but take the middle route of three at the termination of the track by Deep Clough. This stays parallel to the lakeshore but eventually turns left to climb to the marked right of way, which heads northwards to terminate at a metalled lane (GR012776). Turn right along the lane and cross to the far side of the dam, then turn left along the lane towards Fernilee.

Abandon the lane for a water company road which zigzags down to the treatment works by the banks of the Goyt. Beyond the works a gravel track heads northwards before fizzling out in pleasant surroundings where the river meanders beneath a wooded spur.

The path follows the riverbank across fields, crossing a stile at the next field boundary. Several routes converge by a footbridge over the river. This one continues northwards by the river. After a short way it is replaced by a new gravel path, which wanders through Shallcross Wood to meet the outward route close to the footbridge beneath Taxal village. The track to the right climbs out of the valley, back to the car park.

24 Three Shires Head

This walk climbs to no summits. It doesn't see many good rocks, and it's not even much of a challenge. And yet it will pleasantly surprise the walker who doesn't know the area. It's a walk uncluttered with crowds, and route-finding is easy. It visits three counties, and works with the grain of the countryside, following shaded valleys and hollows through high bare moors, heathland, and woodland.

Distance:	**Start/Finish:**
5 miles/8.5km	Car park next to
Height gain:	Clough House,
755 ft/230m	Wildboarclough.
Walking time:	GR987698.
2/3 hours	**Map:**
Type of walk:	OS Outdoor Leisure
Well-defined paths and	24 White Peak or
cart tracks across high	Landranger 118 &
moor and through	119.
moorland valleys.	

The straggling village of Wildboarclough hides from the outside world in a beautiful fertile valley surrounded by high moor. The proud peak of Shutlingsloe, the Cheshire Matterhorn, dominates its scattered cottages and mansions to the west, but this route looks to the eastern moors.

Across the lane at the top of the car park go

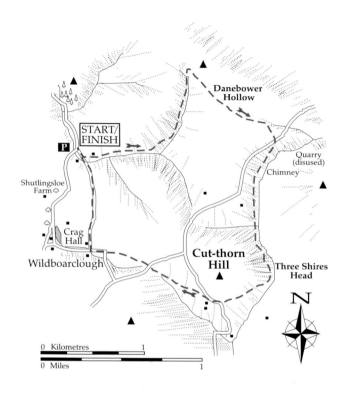

through the gate and follow the eastbound stony track on the southern banks of Cumberland Brook. A wooden footbridge allows the crossing of the stream as the track switches to the northern bank.

The chattering brook cuts itself a deep gorge and is enshrouded by pleasing woodlands. The track climbs steadily high above it in the shade of the woodland and bound by grassy hillslopes to the left. As the woods end beneath Danethorn Hollow, the brook divides, cutting deep ravines into the hillsides. A waterfall tumbles over mossy crags to the right.

The track continues its climb eastwards for about 300yds/m before it divides. A footpath signpost highlights routes to Three Shires Head (right) and the Cat and Fiddle (left). This route follows the latter and climbs north-east, tracing the stream.

There are signs of past mines all around, and the path crosses to the east banks of the stream on a grass-cloaked natural bridge at a point where the stream plummets into an old shaft. At a bend in the stream the path climbs out of the clough and follows a wall to meet a bridleway beneath the brow of Whetstone Ridge.

The Cat and Fiddle lies less than a mile to the north for those in need of refreshment: otherwise turn right and follow the grassy track across the moors – a fence to the left makes a foolproof guide in mist.

The track descends Danebower Hollow to the busy Buxton road above the disused Danebower Quarries. Here slag heaps are largely overgrown with moor grass and just a chimney, some green roads and the ruins of the old barracks remain.

The signposted path across the road down to the quarries lies beyond the crash barriers. It descends steeply to the chimney, crossing a stile by the side of a green road en route. Follow the smooth grassy trackbed of a quarry railway south-west then south into the infant valley of the River Dane. The track degenerates into a footpath, which is wet and rushy in places, though never unpleasantly so. The river flows briskly over its bed of rock slabs.

A stile to the right beneath Holt Farm takes the path across fields but still parallel to the riverbank. The path rejoins the river beyond a third stile at a bend in the river. A grassy cart track descends from Holt Farm to a stone bridge across a side stream and the path joins it at another stile. The narrow track twists through the valley with the hills of bracken and heather closing in on a now livelier stream. Another valley converges from the left and the track comes upon a one-arched bridge and some waterfalls.

This place is Three Shires Head, so called because the counties of Cheshire, Staffordshire and Derbyshire meet here. The bridge, known as Panniers Pool Bridge, was in past centuries used by packhorse trains. From the bridge, stay with the track along the west banks of the Dane, curving round the bouldered escarpment of Cut-thorn Hill. Hen Cloud and the Roaches rise above the green and rolling pasturelands into the southern skies.

After meeting the road at Cut-thorn the route continues on a signposted path to the right of the stone-built cottage. It heads north-west across semi-cultivated fields to renew its acquaintance with the A54. After a shy start, when it bobs beneath the fields, Shutlingsloe rises high on the skyline with its distinctive angular profile.

The path resumes across the road, crosses a wet patch of moor and descends past the ruin of an old farm building towards Leech Wood. A five-bar gate allows entry to the woods, and a stony walled track descends into the shade of pine, larch, rowan and beech. The walker with perfect timing will be able to pick some trackside wild raspberries.

At the bottom of the woods a quiet lane tunnels under more woodland to a junction at the rear of Crag Hall, a grand mansion with lovely gardens. To return to the car park, take the northbound lane (right), which offers exquisite views of Shutlingsloe across the declining pastures of Wildboarclough.

25 Shutlingsloe and Macclesfield Forest

Cheshire hasn't many hills to speak of, and makes a fuss of those within its boundaries. Shutlingsloe is its pride and joy, a shapely peak likened by Patrick Monkhouse to the Matterhorn. Although no Matterhorn, it's a good shapely peak with a few rocks on the top. Circular routes are hard to plan but this one does show off Shutlingsloe's best features and takes in some of the Macclesfield Forest and the attractive pastoral country around Wildboarclough.

Distance:
6 miles/10km
Height gain:
1,345ft/410m
Walking time:
4 hours
Type of walk:
clear paths through forest, moorland and across fields.

Start/Finish:
Trentabank car park, Macclesfield Forest, above Langley. GR962712.
Map: OS Outdoor Leisure 24 White Peak or Landranger 118 & 119.

From the car park, follow the path that runs east between the shores of the Trentabank Reservoir and the road to the roadside lay-by/car park. A footpath, signposted to Wildboarclough and Shutlingsloe, climbs the bank on the opposite side of the road and continues as a well-made stony path through the Macclesfield Forest. Go straight

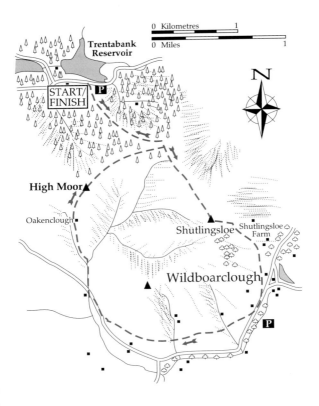

ahead at the crossroads of routes and climb on the flanks of Nessit Hill.

The path bends sharp left at the top edge of the forestry plantation. Ignore the concessionary bridleway signposts to the right, but leave the track shortly after for a path to the right, signposted to

Shutlingsloe. Beyond a stile the now paved path leaves the forest behind and continues south-east across the moors.

Suddenly Shutlingsloe appears, its bold and distinctive crag-fringed summit beckoning the walker to speed up. The last steps to the summit are on a gritstone staircase, surely an unnecessary rebuke to this noble hill. But politics take a back seat for this throne offers wonderful panoramas across Cheshire, Derbyshire and Staffordshire. In the green valley below the scattered cottages of Wildboarclough are framed by hedgerow and copse. Beyond the stately mansion of Crag Hall the eyes rise to the pale hills of Shining Tor and Dane Bower. To the south the ragged Roaches crest promises much for another day, while to the west across rough pastureland the squat hills fade to the Cheshire Plains.

A waymarker on the summit rocks points the way down towards Wildboarclough. The top stretch is a bit of a scramble but the loose path escapes to more gentle slopes. Beyond the first stepstile to the fields surrounding Shutlingsloe Farm, the path is dog-legged to the right. To the south of the farmhouse, it joins a high lane descending south above woodland to the road at Wildboarclough.

Turn right along the road, passing, if you have the willpower, the Crag Inn. A footpath signpost to the right beyond the hostelry points the way across fields. A faint, grassy path threads through hawthorns and gorse bushes, and contours round the hill, gradually veering away from the lane.

The stile in the first cross-wall lies slightly above

the line of the path (ignore the gate). Once over it, the line of the path is unsure, but continue to follow the line of the valley and the next stile, a ladder-stile, will appear. Similarly, three more fields are crossed.

The path changes direction beneath Higher Nabbs Farm, but the sheep have been kind and have shown the way required to cross a stream. In fact their tracks coincide with the route until GR970682 when the sheep evidently lost concentration and headed for a water trough.

The path goes through a gate just a few yards uphill to the right of the trough to join a rutted grassy track. It's not the track shown on the map, but one that eventually descends to Lower Nabbs Farm. Watch out for a stile to the right, which gives access to a metalled track which is the one shown on the map. The track descends to a country lane 200yds/m south of Greenaway Bridge.

Follow the lane to the bridge. A stile on the right marks the start of a footpath heading north up a narrow valley, roughly tracing the east banks of Highmoor Brook and a line of telegraph poles.

Beyond a stepstile the path crosses the brook by a little slabbed footbridge and bears left along the banks of a side stream, Oaken Clough. Waymarks on a telegraph pole offer two routes, one a right of way to Oakenclough Farm, the other a concessionary path avoiding the farmyard. The latter is the preferable route. It crosses the clough and continues on its western banks, eventually passing through newly planted woodland. Some steps take the route on to a farm lane. Oakenclough's substantial stone-built farmhouse lies to the right, across the clough. The marked path climbs the hillsides to the left, guided by a wall and fence for the first part. Shutlingsloe comes back into view to the right as the path passes some pools high on the moor.

Look out for a notice by a wall corner beyond the pools. It shows the route of a concessionary path to be used on the return to the Macclesfield Forest. The path follows the wall north-eastwards on the very edge of High Moor. Beyond a stile in a fence the new route follows a muddy track, which continues along the moorland edge, then veers right along the top edge of the Macclesfield Forest. By now the outward route along the moor to Shutlingsloe will be in full view.

Abandon the track as it turns southwards into the hollow of Highmoor Brook. A stile in the corner of the rough field gives access back to the forest. Ignore the concessionary bridleway, but go right for a few yards to the lower track used earlier in the day. This descends north-west through the forest and back to the car park.

26 Hen Cloud and The Roaches

Of all the places in the book, Hen Cloud and The Roaches probably provide the most spectacular cliffs and wide-sweeping views. Walkers mingle with climbers among overhanging crags. Most books tackle Hen Cloud and The Roaches from the west via Lud's Church. This contrary circular route tackles it from the east, harder going through rough heather dotted with pine, but an escape from the crowds.

Distance:
8 miles/12km
Height gain:
1,700 ft/520m
Walking time:
4/5 hours
Type of walk:
Very rough but rewarding. Difficult traverses through thick heather combined with easy ridge walks.
Start/Finish:
Roaches car park,
Upper Hulme.
GR004622.
Map:
OS Outdoor Leisure 24 White Peak or Landranger 118 & 119.
Note: The car park gets full quite early at peak periods. Rather than clogging up the lanes, use the park-and-ride scheme from nearby Upper Hulme.

It will be tempting to follow the crowds by aiming for The Roaches straight away, but patience will soon be rewarded on a route that will first tackle Hen Cloud, which means high crag. Walk south along the road from the car park before turning left

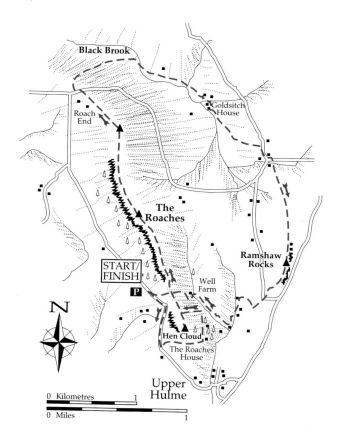

along the drive to The Roaches House. A grassy
path on the right just past the gateposts short-cuts a
large loop in the drive, rejoining it beneath the
soaring cliffs of Hen Cloud. Turn left over a step stile
by the bleak sandstone mansion of the Roaches, and

climb north through woodland. The attractive path surfaces again on the open heather moors east of Hen Cloud. A narrow peaty path furrows westwards through heather and the odd gaunt-looking pine studs the hillside. After a hard slog it attains the ridge, just north of Hen Cloud's summit.

A worthwhile detour over the summit to the southern crags reveals what seems like the rest of England, blurred only by atmospheric haze. It becomes obvious that Hen Cloud is the last bastion of the North, lording it over the plains of the Midlands. The silvery waters of Tittesworth Reservoir glimmer through the haze and distant nameless escarpments pierce the sky.

The route next aims for The Roaches (from the French, *rochers*, meaning rocks) and an obvious path descends the ridge. After scaling two stiles in crosswalls at the col, climb on a wide path to the base of The Roaches' huge crags, which are so popular with climbers. Although a path to the right makes an early bee-line for the ridge, the more interesting route skirts the base of the crags with larch and pine to the left.

After threading between woods and crags, the path veers right to ascend to the ridge, where it becomes a wide path keeping to the right of the crest. This way the interesting views to the west are lost and, unless it is windy or the weather wintry, it is better to pick a way over or near to the rocky crest.

Doxey Pool, a shallow peaty tarn on the ridgetop has a story to tell of a young singing mermaid who was abducted by a group of men. It is said that her ghost still sings here on occasions. Other tales tell of the siting of a huge monster that rose from the deep, or not-so-deep in this case.

Beyond the pool, the path climbs to a trig point, which has its share of interesting rocks with which to frame views of Shutlingsloe. The path now declines to the high road straddling the ridge. Many walkers will be continuing along the ridge, but this route will descend to the Goldsitch area.

The signposted path traces an access lane to a farmhouse. Beyond this it becomes a green track that quickly degenerates into a path. What a fine path it is, meandering generally eastwards down hillslopes of heather and bracken down to Black Brook, a name that betrays the coal-mining heritage of the area. A decaying footbridge of concrete and steel carries the path across the brook. The waymarked route now climbs the far banks to high fields south of Moss End Farm.

A wooden post shows the direction of two footpaths. Ignore the one to the left, but carry on south-east across fields, keeping roughly parallel with the line of Black Brook. After scaling a couple of stiles the path aims for a group of buildings, eventually reaching a stony access drive left of Goldsitch House.

Maintain direction across the drive by going though the stile ahead and cross more fields towards the depot of a 4x4 vehicle dealer. A footpath signpost on the farm lane encountered beyond a five-bar gate marks the various routes. This route follows a short concessionary path to the right along the lane, then left towards the depot.

The well-waymarked right of way that follows has been diverted round the perimeter of the depot and can be a little overgrown with thistles in summer. Any difficulties, however, are short-lived and the path traverses fields with the spiky Ramshaw Rocks directly ahead.

The path turns left along a sunken track, which leads to the road by Newstone Farm (GR017638). At the T-junction, go a short way south along the road to a footpath sign and post that show the way towards Ramshaw Rocks. The path, initially unclear underfoot, goes south-east across cow-pocked fields to a stile. Beyond the stile it continues across heathland, aiming for the rocks. Tussocks of grass that hide in the heather make the narrow path a little hazardous for the unwary. The author was tossed on to his haunches on one occasion and forced into further undignified manoeuvres.

The path reaches the ridge by some rocks and joins a prominent track (bridleway) at GR021629. It follows the track across bilberry and heather by the ridge wall and veers right with it for a short way. Leave the track at a footpath signpost 'To Ramshaw Rocks' and climb back to the ridge through more heather. A good route weaves through the grit-stone giving wide views back to the crests of Hen Cloud and The Roaches to the west, and the high settlements on Morridge to the east.

On descending to the road, the rights of way are not ingrained on the terrain. This is open access though and the route makes its way across heather and by crag (not shown on the map) to the looping farm lane that is shown on current Landrangers but not on the Outdoor Leisure Map.

The tarred farm lane descends to Ferny Knowe. (It is not the one that is shown to Naychurch.) Keep the large farmhouse and yard to the right and go straight ahead on a track passing in front of a new stone-built house. Here the surfacing ends and a grassy track descends to the right behind an outbuilding to cross a small stream by a stile. The track continues beneath some wooden pylons to reach a crossroads of tracks by some woodland.

Turn right on a stony farm track towards Well Farm. At first only a derelict stone farmhouse is visible beneath The Roaches' crags, but the occupied lower farm soon appears. Turn left over a stile preceding the farmyard to cross a field to another stile by an 'open country' sign. Turn right across tussocky grassland by the perimeter wall of the access area. A path begins as the route veers west to climb to the col between Hen Cloud and The Roaches.

Turn right at the col towards The Roaches to cross a stile in a wall and follow the path north-west to the next stile. Beyond this, a clear track skirting The Roaches' southern crags descends west to the road near to the car park.

The Eastern Edges

Dividing the River Derwent from the populated fringes of Sheffield, the eastern edges offer some of the best ridge walks in the Dark Peak.

From the northern outlier, Outer Edge to Back Tor the ridge is wide and boggy, rather akin to the terrain encountered on the Pennine Way. Here long approaches from Langsett and the Strines areas offer remote ways to the sullen tops.

The Derwent Edges show more rock to the skies, and glimpses of the string of reservoirs in the valley. The rock really shows itself properly beyond Moscar, where the gritstone cliffs of Stanage Edge parade themselves above Hathersage and Bamford.

These places are at their finest in late summer when the heather and bracken add a patchwork quilt of colour to the cold grey rocks. The further south, the brighter the colours, reaching a crescendo by the attractive woodlands beneath the Froggatt and Curbar Edges.

The gigantic slabs and outcrops of millstone grit have found favour with climbers and many famous names have started their craft here. On most weekends the walker, the sightseer and the climber co-exist on these fine skyline terraces.

27 Howden Edge

A stroll along the firm terrain of the Howden Edge between Wet Stones and Margery Hill reveals some of the Peak's finest views with relative ease of walking. The sting in this tail, however, comes with the trek northwards from the Cut Gate Path, where tracks lose themselves in the mosses and peat-hagged terrain of Outer Edge and Stainery Clough Head.

Distance:	**Start/Finish:**
13 miles/20km	Fairholmes
Height gain:	Information Centre.
1,345ft/410m	GR173893.
Walking time:	**Note:**
7 hours	The walk is over an
Type of walk:	access area which can
Strenuous high	be closed on shooting
moorland walk with	days between August
stretches of tough	12 and December 10
trackless terrain.	and also at times of
	high fire risk.

From the north end of Fairholmes car park, follow a metalled lane that curves to the right beneath the Derwent dam. Leave it for a left turn on a flinted track which climbs through the trees, past the dam, and along the eastern shores of the reservoir.

The track contours round the entrance to Abbey Brook Clough and heads for the Howden dam, but leave it on the crown of the bend at GR171922 for a stony, bulldozed track climbing north-east through birch woods. Beyond a gate it leaves the woodland for coarse, grassy moorland slopes high above Abbey Brook, which delves deep into the hillsides.

As it gains height and breaks free from the confines of stone walls, the track becomes less distinct. Take the left fork, which swings northwards before descending to a saddle of high moor bridging the gap between Abbey Brook Clough and Howden Clough. From here a steep climb follows to the main ridge near the Wet Stones. Climb northwards along the firm, grassy ridge, which is now speckled with bilberry, but still very green compared to the dark heather moors in other directions. The wide groove of a boundary ditch flecked with cotton grass joins the path from the right and accompanies it along the ridge to High Stones, where a small cairn marks the summit.

From the rocky edge the hillside plummets to a shelf of high moorland, cut deep by Cranberry and Howden Cloughs. The shelf, in turn, plummets into the upper Derwent valley, where the reservoirs peep out through the trees. Beyond all this the heather-clad moors of Bleaklow stretch to the north and west horizons, while to the south-west, the more shapely hummocks of Edale's Back Tor and Mam Tor highlight the great ridge above Edale.

The best path northwards keeps to the stony edge overlooking Cranberry Clough. Ahead Margery Hill's rocks (the Margery Stones) look less interesting, but its summit has a trig point to be touched and a new view across the plains of West Yorkshire.

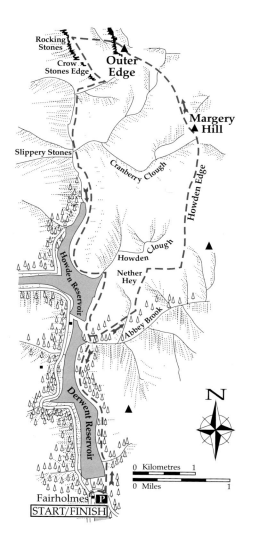

Accordingly a path diverts to the top and rejoins the edge a short way to the north-west.

The odd wooden stake marks the path north to the Cut Gate path, which is an ancient traders' route linking Penistone with the Derwent Valley. Hereabouts it is a deep groove in the hillside and marked by a large pile of stones. By now the edge path struggles to get a hold in the peaty ground that rises to Outer Edge. The route is rarely in doubt: a series of stakes continues across the rough terrain and a blurred dark line highlights the bootprints of past walkers (not always co-inciding with the stakes). The walker has to deviate to avoid the worst of the deep peat groughs – it's hard going.

The summit itself is quite firm and marked by a trig point. To the east crags and boulders fringe the escarpment's edge lending a little shape where there seemed to be none. To the north, in the mid-distance, cars speed by on the busy A628 trans-Pennine road. Beyond it further moorland climbs to Holme Moss where the radio mast reaches for the sky.

A path of sorts continues along the watershed above Stainery Clough Head, but leave this one to the masochists. Instead, head west to the edge, where a little path winds through the rocks to descend to a wet, grassy plateau. A faint path traverses the plateau crossing just one deep peat grough on its way to the Crow Stones.

This second and more impressive group of rocks, surrounded by bilberry and heather, offers a fine spot for a break, as do the nearby Rocking Stones. The upper

Derwent valley, now free from the conifer plantations and reservoirs, meanders through the moors, overlooked by the rock-fringed heathery peaks of Horse Stone Naze and Barrow Stones. There are no paths from Crow Stones back to the Derwent valley, although a little sheep track does head north to the waterfall on Stainery Clough (about GR168977). The descent of the clough is a bit of a scramble and doesn't come recommended by the author. It would be safer and easier to walk southwards through the deep heather slopes beneath the Crow Stones to pick up the old shooters' track in Broadhead Clough. This in turn descends to the main upper Derwent valley track at GR172963, close to a footbridge across Broadhead Clough's stream. The track leads the route south above the twin-arched stone bridge across the River Derwent at Slippery Stones.

This is the original 17th-century bridge that spanned the river at Derwent village before its flooding for Ladybower Reservoir. It was removed stone by stone and reconstructed here in 1959, after the fund-raising efforts of Sheffield author and journalist, John Derry.

Beyond Slippery Stones the path climbs on the grassy slopes of Cold Side before entering coniferous woodlands that fringe the headwaters of the Howden Reservoir. It follows the reservoir's sinuous shoreline round Cow Hey, and past the Howden dam, beyond which it meets the outward route. Trace the route south, past the Derwent dam and back along the metalled lane to Fairholmes.

28 Back Tor and Strines

Back Tor is the high point of a walk along Derwent Edge from Fairholmes or from the Ladybower Inn. Approaches from the east are less used, largely because they are longer and take in less of the ridge itself. The ancient tracks through the heather from the Strines Inn and Hurkling Edge can be combined in a fascinating circular walk that not only includes this rocky top, but also some very attractive woodland and pasture.

Distance:
11 miles/18km
Height gain:
1,690ft/515m
Walking time:
7 hours
Type of walk:
Moderate to strenuous with many ups and downs in the later stages. Terrain varies from heathery moorland ridges to field paths and woodland tracks.

Start/Finish:
Car park, Hurkling Edge. GR246945.
Note:
The walk is over a permitted access area, which can be closed on shooting days between August 12 and December 10 and at times of high fire risk.

Heather-clad Hurkling Edge climbs gradually to the skyline, looking down on the trees and bracken fields of Agden Valley's upper reaches. The bridleway to be followed, known as Dukes Road, is a wide, well-defined track along the crest. A line of shooting butts to the left reminds the walker that this is an active grouse moor. As the route gains height, the valley shallows, the trees lose their grip in the heather, and the track veers south-west towards the main Derwent ridge. South of Round Hill, a signpost marks the track's change of status from bridleway to footpath. Not far beyond the signpost the path joins the main north-south ridge route – a large pile of stones highlights the spot.

Abbey Brook snakes through grassy spurs to the environs of the Derwent valley, which is invisible from hereabouts. To the north dull moorland swells to Margery Hill where a few rocks crown the summit. To the south, Back Tor's crinkly rock-bound top just peeps out from behind the scabby top of Cartledge Bents.

Turn south to follow the path across damp grassy moorland over Cartledge Bents, later veering south-south-west to the summit of Back Tor. Here huge slabs of gritstone upthrust to the skies. A trig point mounted on one of them offers a good leaning spot to admire the views across the reservoirs to Bleaklow and Kinder, and back to Stanage Edge and the Mam Tor ridge.

Head south from the summit to Bradfield Gate Head, where a tall boundary stone marks an intersection of paths. Turn left along a wide path known as the Foulstone Road. It descends between the heather fields of Foulstone Moor and Brogging Moss. Halfway down it becomes a stony vehicle track that heads for some conifer plantations north of Strines Reservoir.

Beyond a gate at the plantation's edge a tarred estate lane leads through the shade of the trees to the road near Strines Bridge. Those with a thirst or a need for a bar meal could make a detour right and uphill to the Strines public house. Otherwise turn left, following the road to GR227909, where a stony track descends to Strines Reservoir.

A stone-built tower, Boot's Folly, protrudes from the pastured hillsides opposite. Unlike most follies it was not built on the whim of an over-rich landowner, but to provide his workforce with jobs to see them through hard times. At Brogging Farm a signpost on a pole points the way across fields down to the foot of the Strines dam. Beyond a stile the path enters pleasant woodland at its foot, crosses a stream via a footbridge, and traces the banks to the head of a second reservoir, Dale Dike.

Dale Dike was the scene of Britain's worst reservoir disaster. The original earth-fill dam collapsed soon after being built in 1864 and before the reservoir had filled completely. The roaring torrents devastated the village of Low Bradfield and the Loxley valley, killing over 244 people and destroying over 500 houses. The centreline of the original dam has been marked with stone posts.

The path divides. The left fork, not a right of way, follows the reservoir shores. The right fork is, and climbs the stile in a wall to the right, then wades through bracken before veering north-east across high pastureland parallel to the lake. The route, which is well waymarked by the arrows of the Sheffield Country Walk at stiles and gateposts in the field boundaries, reveals fine views of the verdant countryside. The path enters the shade of a conifer wood. At a stile and divergence of paths, the Sheffield Country Walk takes the right fork. Today's route descends left to follow a path between crumbling walls of moss-covered stone. It meets the shoreline path and turns right along it to pass the reservoir pumphouse and the dam. It continues through more woodland and descends on a series of steps to meet a stony track which descends further to cross Dale Dike on a wide wooden bridge.

The track climbs further through the woods to join

an overgrown lane from the dam, which brings the route to Dale Road. Note the memorial to those killed by the breaching of the dam. It stands on the right, not far from the exit. Turn right along the country lane then leave it after 100yds/m for a bridleway climbing north over scrubland dappled with bracken, foxgloves and the odd tree. On reaching a gate, the bridleway becomes a thistle-lined, reedy cart track that passes beneath some wooden pylons before ending at Mortimer Road.

Turn right along the road and take the right fork, passing Wilkin Hall, a rather grandly-named stone cottage that is now an outdoor pursuits centre. Just beyond it a signposted path, which quickly establishes itself as a leafy track, descends to cross Emlin Dike on a substantial stone bridge. Go straight on at the crossroads of paths at GR250929, close to Agden House. The path winds through patches of bracken before re-entering the wood-land, this section belonging to the Agden Bog Nature Reserve.

The path crosses Agden Dike on a footbridge and turns right, close to the shoreline of Agden Reservoir, whose waters are obscured by the trees. At a gate and adjacent stile, the path should be abandoned for one that doubles back north-north-east, squeezed between the line of a stone wall and the edge of a conifer plantation. The path turns sharp right and climbs along the plantation's northern perimeter at Agden Side. The heather-clad slopes are steep, but in late summer the bilberries at the side of the path may compensate and refresh the weary walker.

Turn left on reaching the stone wall at the top of the bank. Here a delightful path traces the upper edge of the Agden valley. The tree-filled valley bottom scythes through heather moorland with the sleek hillslopes of Hurkling Edge cutting a dash at its head.

The path meets Agden Side Road. Across the high country lane a ladder-stile marks the start of the next path across Cowell Flat. Following the line of some pylons for a few strides, it meets a more prominent path heading north-west parallel to the road. Keep to the right of the tall stone walls enclosing some cow pastures. The path soon enters attractive open heather moorland studded with scrub birch. For somewhere so close to the road it seems remote.

The path ends without warning back at the well-concealed car park and the start of the walk.

29 The Derwent Edges

One of the classic walks in the Peak, this route along the Derwent Edges takes the walker on a promenade through heather and gritstone to a multitude of distinctive weatherbeaten rocks and tors. Beginning from Ashopton, it soon gets to grips with the ridge on Whinstone Lee Tor, and greedily takes in all the views from the tops before descending to the shores of the Derwent Reservoir. From here it strolls to journey's end through the wooded valley and past the ghosts of sunken villages.

Distance:
10 miles/16km
Height gain:
1,180ft/360m
Walking time:
6 hours
Type of walk:
Moderate walk on
moorland paths.
Start/Finish:
Ladybower Reservoir,

Ashopton. GR195864.
Roadside car park
50yds/m east.
Note:
The walk is over an
area which can be
closed on shooting
days between August
12 and December 10
and also at times of
high fire risk.

The walk begins on a metalled private road that zigzags past a few of Ashopton's remaining cottages. Where the road terminates in a walled area go through the gate to the left and double back up the hillside on a forestry track climbing through pines and larches. The track, which can be muddy in winter, leaves the forest and continues its steady climb beneath the precipitous bracken-cloaked sides of Lead Hill. The zigzag to the ridge shown on the map has been replaced by a well-worn direct climb. Here the route abandons the bridleway to climb to the rocks of Whinstone Lee Tor.

Kinder Scout has, by this time, surfaced above the rocky crowns of Crook Hill, and glowers across Edale at the Mam Tor ridge. To the south the gritstone cliffs of Stanage and Bamford Edge fringe their heathery escarpments.

The ridge path embarks upon a steady climb that will culminate on Back Tor. Outside the summer months it can be quite sticky, a dark ribbon of peaty mud slurping through the heather and mosses.

A series of gritstone tors and outcrops lines these Derwent Edges: firstly the Hurkling Stones, then, after crossing the path from Ladybower to Moscar, the more impressive Wheel Stones. The latter are sometimes referred to as the Coach and Horses. They stand watch on their heathery top like a huddled group of tubby soldiers.

Beyond the Wheel Stones the path climbs over White Tor and another group of rocks overlooking the cavernous hollow of Mill Brook. Beneath Ladybower's waters hereabouts are the remains of Derwent village. The walk climbs past the 500m contour for the first time on Dovestone Tor, where a line of broken cliffs fringe the moor. Beyond them is a group of rounded outcrops known as the Cakes of Bread. From here large gritstone flags have been laid across the glutinous peat.

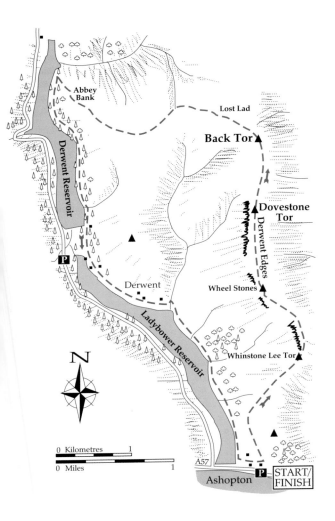

Abbey
Bank

Lost Lad

Back Tor ▲

Derwent Reservoir

**Dovestone
Tor** ▲

Derwent Edges

P

▲

Derwent

Wheel Stones ▲

Ladybower Reservoir

Whinstone Lee Tor ▲

N

▲

0 Kilometres   1

0 Miles   1

A57

Ashopton   P   START/
FINISH

161

The final short climb of the day leads the walker to the bold gritstone summit of Back Tor. Its trig point stands on a huge weather-rounded boulder and offers wide views over the reservoirs, across to Bleaklow and Kinder. Stanage and the Mam Tor ridge complete the southern vista.

After scrambling off the summit, continue along the flagged path descending north-west to a subsidiary top. The top, known as Lost Lad, relates how a young shepherd boy who had gone to the hills to bring down the remainder of his flock after a snow storm was then stranded in another blizzard. After wandering for many hours he found a boulder under which to shelter. Before crawling in he scrawled a message on a stone, which he placed on top of the boulder. He succumbed to the cold and perished that night, but it was many months before his message was discovered. It read simply, 'lost lad'.

The flags cease and the path plunges down a deep groove on some steep slopes. The gradient eases on Green Stiches and the route continues as a lightly-grooved grassy track. Heather is now confined to patches among the pale windswept grasses.

Leave the track at GR182911 for a path forking right to a clearly visible ladder-stile and footpath fingerpost. The path continues north-westwards down a grassy spur before turning right by a dilapidated wall. Here it descends to a meeting of footpaths near the ruins of Bamford House. Another signpost marks the spot.

It is feasible to descend directly on steep slopes to the Derwent Reservoir, but a better way turns right following a wall down Abbey Bank. The final stretch of the latter path passes through a gap in the wall before tracing a deep channel through thick heather down to the conifers of the Abbey Tip Plantation. Here it descends further through the woods to the wide track near the reservoir shores.

Turn left and follow the track past the Derwent dam. Those in need of sustenance could make a detour to Fairholmes where they could get beverages and maybe a hot pie. Otherwise continue on the track to the metalled lane running along the east side of Ladybower Reservoir. The quiet lane passes pleasant cottages that were once on the outskirts of Derwent village.

The lane terminates at the bridge over Mill Beck. In times of drought the crumbled walls and foundations of the village surface on the crazed mud. A notice shows the positions of Derwent Hall, the old post office, school, church and some of the old cottages. A small bridge is still intact, but the village folk dismantled the larger twin-arched packhorse bridge stone by stone and rebuilt it at Slippery Stones higher up the valley.

Continue on a well-graded track southwards along the shores of the reservoir. After rounding Grainfoot Clough it passes beneath woodlands with the rocks of Whinstone Lee Tor crowning the hilltop. Finally it meets the outward route above the Ashopton viaduct, just 100yds/m from the car park.

30 Stanage Edge and High Neb

Probably the finest approaches to Stanage Edge begin from Hathersage or Longshaw. However, the one from the A57 at Moscar Lodge offers an easy but rewarding high edge route suitable for a summer evening stroll or when time is short.

Distance:	*firm footpaths, mainly*
5 miles/8km	*alongside the cliffs.*
Height gain:	***Start/Finish:***
560ft/170m	*Roadside car park on*
Walking time:	*A57 at Moscar Lodge*
2/3 hours	*GR231879.*
Type of walk:	
An easy walk along	

The busy A57 road climbs to Moscar, its last Pennine moor before descending to the city of Sheffield. A small roadside car park is conveniently sited south of Moscar Lodge at the start of the walk.

Beyond a gate close to the car park, the wide path makes a bee-line across reedy moorland towards the rounded hill that is Stanage End. On gaining height the terrain becomes more bouldery, and a little heather merges with the grass and reeds. The track divides beneath the old quarries of Stanage End: either could be used, but save the best until last and take the right fork. The path climbs over bracken-cloaked moorland beneath the edge. Crags replace boulders. With each footstep they become

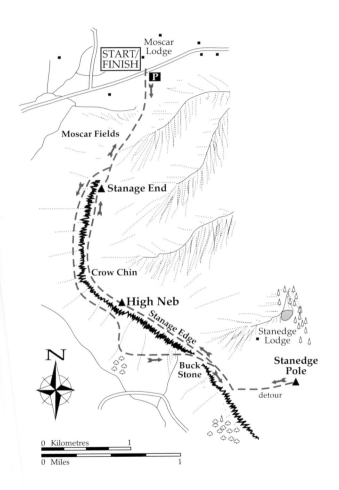

START/FINISH

Moscar
Lodge

P

Moscar Fields

▲ Stanage End

Crow Chin

▲ High Neb

Stanage Edge

Stanedge
Lodge

Buck
Stone

Stanedge
Pole

detour

N

0 Kilometres 1

0 Miles 1

larger, more impressive and much more interesting to the climbing fraternity. As the little path rounds the protruding crags of Crow Chin, the moorland below has risen to a marshy saddle between Moscar and Bamford Moors. On meeting a little path that has descended from High Neb, turn right, downhill to meet a wide fenced track close to a small wood. Turn left along the track which passes close to the Buck Stone, a gigantic slab of rock. Once used as a staging post by the packhorse trains that straddled the moors, the Buck Stone had a shelter built into it. Continue along the track, which now climbs back towards the ridge, this time to the top. The paved path arcing down through Stanage Plantations is Jacob's Ladder, not to be confused with the Jacob's Ladder at Edale.

A detour could be made along the Long Causeway to Stanedge Pole where views would encompass Sheffield and the wide plains of southern Yorkshire. Alternatively trend left along the ridge to the rocky summit of High Neb, the high point of the day.

Numbered rock basins line the route along the top. The basins were neatly sculpted by gamekeepers at the turn of the century to keep the grouse watered.

On a sunny August evening the rocks turn to a warm gold and the purple heather turns to fiery red in the glow of sunset. The walker could, in his or her own time, amble back along the ridge path watching the light fade behind the pyramidal Win Hill and the serrated tors of the Derwent Edges, returning to the car park at dusk.

31 Stanage Edge from Hathersage

The gritstone teeth of Stanage Edge fringe the skyline above Hathersage, that gateway to the peak for the people of Sheffield. Although most of the population walk the Edge from one of the high car parks it surely would be better from a purist's point of view to walk from the valley. This route does just that, following unsurfaced lanes through farmland with those crags always in view and getting nearer.

Distance: 6miles/11km	A moderate walk with steady climbs on unsurfaced lanes and paths to the ridge.
Height gain: 985ft/300m	
Walking time: 4 hours	**Start/Finish:** Car park, Hathersage. GR232812.
Type of walk:	

The walk begins on Baulk Lane by the side of the Hathersage Inn. The lane climbs steadily north, passing the cricket ground, where they sell teas on match days, and a few houses before entering a bowl of green pastures fringed by the distant crags of Stanage. As the lane leaves the buildings behind, the Tarmac loses its hold and it becomes an unsurfaced track. On the approach to Cowclose Farm take the signposted left fork past Brookfield Manor to a country lane (GR233832). Turn right along the lane then left on a drive that climbs to North Lees Hall.

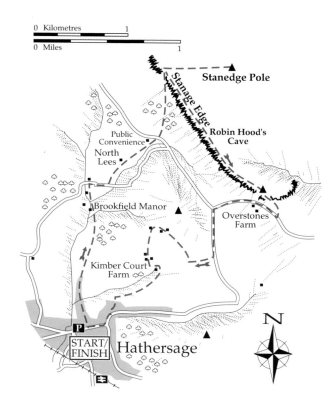

The 16th-century castellated building, now an agricult-
ural school, was once home to the catholic Eyre family and
was an inspiration for Charlotte Brontë's Jane Eyre. The
authoress stayed in Hathersage for a few weeks in 1895.
In the 17th-century the Eyres were driven out by the
Protestant community and the remains of a chapel, built
in 1685 only to be destroyed three years later, can still be
seen in the grounds.

After rounding the hall turn right up some steps to cut the corner to another track that traverses hillside pastures before seeking the shade of some attractive mixed woodland. A stepped path to the left makes a short cut to the roadside toilets and mountain rescue hut at GR239837.

Now the gritstone edges are much closer. Slightly staggered to the right, a grassy path heads for them, joining a path from the nearby car park. A causey path, paved with weather-beaten millstone grit slabs, climbs through the woodland of Stanage Plantation before veering left and making an assault on the cliffs.

Once on the edge, a detour on the prominent track across the heather moor to Stanedge Pole is worthwhile for those with extra time and the will to see the conurbation of Sheffield spread across the eastern plains. Otherwise head south along the airy cliff edges above Robin Hood's Cave, where the legendary outlaw perhaps hid while on the run from the Sheriff of Nottingham.

The path continues above the climbers' crags to a jagged bouldery summit capped by a concrete trig point. It offers views down the hollowed scoop overlooked by the Burbage Rocks and shapely Higger Tor. A path continues east to the high road at Upper Burbage Bridge where strong walkers could descend by Higger Tor and Carl Wark.

An easier alternative retraces steps to the well-defined path that descends from 100yds/m west of the trig point to the same road near Overstones Farm.

Turn right along it and take the left fork downhill to GR245824, where a stony farm lane heads west before arcing round the high fields and farms of Leveret Croft and Kimber Court. (NB The more direct path shown descending past Toothill Farm is overgrown and obstructed close to the farmhouse.)

At a gate preceding Moorseats Farm the path is diverted from the lane diagonally across fields to the left. It joins another track, rounding Carr Head Farm before descending as a sunken tree-lined lane to the original Hathersage settlement. This huddled around the ancient earthworks of Camp Green and the spired parish church where Little John is said to have been buried.

A short downhill walk leads to the main road and the modern village centre.

32 Burbage Rocks and Carl Wark

When days are short, when there is only an afternoon to spare or you want to spend an evening after work on spectacular hillsides, this walk should be considered. It is a fine mix of heather, crag and bracken. Late afternoon or evening sunlight can set the colours aflame, especially in August when the heather glows pink. For a short walk it packs plenty of detail – two little hills, one with an Iron Age fort; one long rim of climbers' cliffs; a packhorse bridge; some waterfalls and an imposing mansion.

Distance:
5 miles/8km
Height gain:
755ft/230m
Walking time:
3 hours
Type of walk:
Fairly easy walk on moorland paths and tracks.
Start/Finish:
Longshaw NT car park by Fox House Inn. GR267801.
Note:
This walk could be extended to include Stanage Edge.

In 1927 the Duke of Rutland put his Longshaw Estate up for sale. It had been considered a fine grouse moor but also included the lodge and its carefully planned grounds and woodland. A charity was set up and the land donated to the National Trust who kept it open for the public. This walk takes full advantage of the freedom of the estate and climbs from the lodge to the heights.

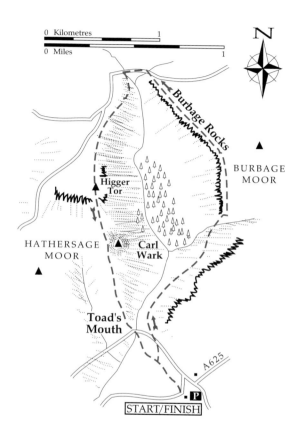

Take the narrow path from the back of the car park heading southwards. Turn right at the junction with an unsurfaced lane, following the signs to the Longshaw Visitor Centre. The main lodge, an impressive gothic building of darkened millstone grit, has now been turned into apartments.

Turn right again at the visitor centre following the drive to the B-road where a footpath signpost to the left points the way through woodland. In spring the woodland carpets are splashed with the purple of the common dog violet, the yellow of lesser celandine, and the delicate shades of wood sorrel. A right fork leads to the A-road immediately opposite the footpath known as the Duke of Rutland's Drive.

This old green road (there is not much green left now) slips into an amphitheatre of heather and gritstone. On one side are the cliffs of the Burbage Rocks, on the other, the craggy knolls of Carl Wark and Higger Tor.

Duke's Drive chooses a low route beneath Burbage Rocks. It may sound unexciting, but it retains the feeling of walking through this great arena with Carl Wark towering into the sky.

After a short while a little packhorse bridge comes into view. Shaded by the conifers that bask around Burbage Brook, the surroundings look ideal for a picnic and well-used paths do go down to it. But this route aims for higher things and, on meeting the right of way from the old bridge, it follows a peaty path from the road through the heather to the main skyline route.

The path descends hereabouts to cross a little stream but it soon gets back to the rocky edge where climbers play all day on solid gritstone buttresses. The path terminates at a roadside stile.

On weekends there will be crowds and their cars. Some come to climb; some stop for a cup of tea or an ice cream with a view provided by the sales van; but most to do the short and easy walk to Higger Tor and Carl Wark.

Higger Tor, or Higher Tor, is the next objective. Strong walkers could incorporate some of Stanage Edge with this route by heading west across the heather moor past Cowper Stone. After a descent from the clifftop by the Long Causeway through Stanage Plantation, high lanes would then take the route to GR247818. Here a winding track climbs past Callow to another lane at the 372 spot height where a short stroll leads to Higger Tor's summit.

On the main route, after turning left along the road to the high car park, a stile gives access for a return to the moors. There are two paths. The higher one is best, choosing to head southwards across the heather. After dipping slightly at Fiddler's Elbow, the path climbs on an eroded course to the top of this shapely gritstone hill.

The splendid little summit has enough rocks and bouldered perches to seat the masses and plenty of nature's own sculptures to inspire the budding Henry Moore. Carl Wark, a squat, rakish knoll rises from the bracken and heather luring the walker onwards. The path scrambles between rocks and continues across bracken towards Carl Wark before the easy climb to this second and lower rocky tor.

The summit is a former fort, which historians once believed to be of Iron Age origins. They now think it dates back to around the 7th-century. The hill's natural fortifications were enhanced by the laying of huge rocks, creating a 10ft/3m rampart along the only weakness.

The path descends from the south-western tip, weaving through bracken. A fork to the left descending to the forest and the previously mentioned packhorse bridge would be perfectly feasible and attractive but would involve retracing the outward route along the Duke of Rutland's Drive. It would, therefore, be better to continue on the intermittent path southwards past the rocks known as Toad's Mouth to the A-road.

Across the road a path descends into the woodlands of the Longshaw Estate to cross the Burbage Brook. It climbs past some waterfalls to meet the outward route in the middle of the woods, where steps should be retraced to the visitor centre and back to the car park.

33 Curbar and Froggatt Edges

Although not the shortest, this lofty circular walk is probably the easiest in the book. Beginning in the parklands of the Longshaw Estate it takes to the gritstone edges and heather moors high above the woodlands and emerald fields of the Derwent valley. The first, White Edge, is the highest and offers views across heath and shimmering grasslands to the plains of Yorkshire.

Distance:
8 miles/13km
Height gain:
260ft/80m
Walking time:
3/4 hours
Type of walk:
A very easy walk that keeps to the high ground on paths along

the gritstone edges.
Start/Finish:
Longshaw NT car park by Fox House Inn. GR267801.
Map: OS Outdoor Leisure 24 White Peak. The car park is on the OS Outdoor Leisure 1 Dark Peak.

Follow the path from the back of the car park towards the National Trust centre, turning left at the T-junction before Longshaw Lodge. The stony lane veers south through woods to join a grassy track beyond one of the estate's white gates. Turn right along the track beneath bouldery slopes, to a junction of high country lanes on Totley Moss.

Across the road, ignore the signposted bridleway at

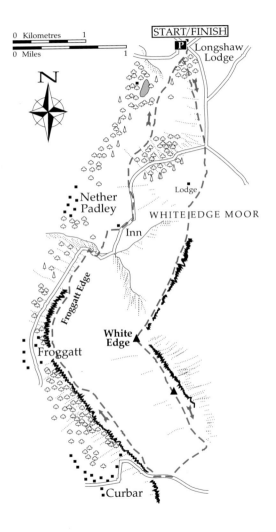

the first gate, but go to a stile a few yards further. This marks the beginning of a permissive path, not shown on current OS Outdoor Leisure maps but shown as black dashes on the Landranger. The well-defined path heads south across the moors. On dark days, White Edge Lodge on the right is an eerie sight standing gaunt and alone in the middle of high moorland.

After passing copses of pine on White Edge Moor, the path heads for Hurkling Rocks on White Edge, passing through a gap in a stone cross wall. On the higher ground to the left prolific heather mixes with swaying moor grass and the views across it extend as far east into Yorkshire as the atmosphere will allow. Signs ask that walkers keep to the path, for this is a wildlife sanctuary. To the west the hill slopes fall away to the lower rocks of Froggatt Edge. By the edge they are decorated with heather, bracken and boulder, with birch and rowan adding a little extra colour.

Beyond some enclosed pastures the path leaves the edge. It veers south-west down rough grassy slopes, crosses a plank bridge over Sandyford Brook to meet a rough track that leads to a roadside car park at Curbar Gap (GR262747).

Some steps at the west end of the car park take the route out on to Curbar Edge. A wide track stays about 30yds/m from the edge, but a more entertaining route stays closer to the rocks.

Looking south the cliffs of the Baslow Edge overlook the Derwent valley where small villages – Curbar, Calver,

Baslow and Stoney Middleton – are surrounded by emerald pastures, woods and rolling hillsides. There are also some of the best rock climbs in the Peak hereabouts. On most days the cliffs will echo to the sound of climbers' voices. Inland the heather is profuse, as is the forest cover beneath the edge.

The paths bend right and the cliffs change their name, to Froggatt Edge. Gigantic blocks of rock jut out from the woodland and another village, Grindleford, comes into view far below. A path diverts right to visit a Bronze Age Circle, but the main route enters woodland before descending to a kissing gate at the roadside. A short way east along the road the path to be followed descends to ford a stream and enters Hay Wood, where it passes to the left of a car park.

Look out for a small gate in the wall to the right. It is the start of a faint path that cuts diagonally across fields to the Grouse Inn, which is always in view. Turn left along the road past the inn. Ignore the signposted path just beyond the inn, but leave the road for a stony lane heading north into the grounds of the Longshaw Country Park.

To the left fields decline to the tree-filled Padley Gorge. A signpost diverts walkers from the track to a path that passes through fields to the right of the lodge before rejoining it by the information centre, where there is a cafe and toilets. Turn right beyond the centre, then left, following the signposted track to the car park.

34 Langsett to Hathersage

I didn't find a satisfactory circular walk to explore the Langsett Moors. The Cut Gate path made a fine ascent route to Margery Hill, but there were no other rights of way back to base. My answer is to see it at its best, on a linear walk. Being a hard taskmaster I've added an extra day, so now it's a long distance walk taking in some of the best sights in the Dark Peak. I chose Hathersage as the finishing point for its bus and railway connections with Manchester and Sheffield, while Langsett is served by buses from Barnsley.

Distance: 30 miles/45km	**Finish:** Hathersage. GR230815.
Walking time: 2 days	**Maps:** OS Outdoor Leisure
Type of walk: A long tough two-day walk over moorland.	Dark and White Peak; Landranger 118 & 119; Harvey's Superwalker Dark Peak North and South.
Start: Langsett Barn Car Park. GR212004.	

Day 1: 16miles/26km (13miles/21km to youth hostel)

From the back of the Langsett Barn Car Park, follow the path into the Langsett Bank plantations where pine and larch predominate. Take the left fork and follow the waymarking arrows on a path

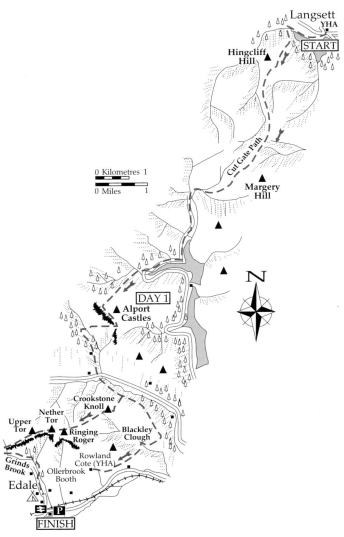

Langsett
YHA
START

Hingcliff Hill ▲

Cut Gate Path

Margery Hill ▲

0 Kilometres 1

0 Miles 1

▲

▲

DAY 1

Alport ▲ Castles

N

▲

▲

Crookstone Knoll ▲

Upper Tor ▲
Nether Tor ▲ ▲ Ringing Roger

Blackley Clough

Grinds Brook

Rowland Cote (YHA)

Ollerbrook Booth

Edale

FINISH

181

that zigzags down to follow the shoreline of Lang-sett Reservoir, which is often colonised by a wide variety of birdlife. Beyond the north-west end of the lake, the path meets the Cut Gate path, a wide track, once used by farmers from the Hope and Derwent valleys to take their livestock to the market at Penistone.

The Cut Gate path descends south to cross the Porter or Little Don River on the one-arched, stone-built Brookhouse Bridge (GR197006 – not named on the maps) before winding up the hill at the edge of the forest and across Hingcliff Common. It traces Mickleden Edge above a pleasantly wooded moor-land valley, but soon there is more moorland than valley and the walk cuts through peatlands to the main ridge. Margery Hill is just a stone's throw away for those who want an early peak.

The Cut Gate path now descends into the Derwent valley, meandering into the tight recesses of Cranberry Clough before veering left to the bridge at Slippery Stones. The bridge once spanned Mill Brook in the heart of Derwent village before its flooding for Ladybower Reservoir. Cross the bridge and follow the track through more forests. The track continues as a metalled lane beyond a car park and traces the shoreline of Howden Reservoir.

Turn right along the flinted road at the forest gate (GR155927). Just beyond the crossing of the Ditch Clough stream, turn left on a track signposted to Alport Castles. It strikes boldly up the hillside, through trees at first, then on the open moor to reach the Castles.

The path into the Alport valley begins to the south-east of the castles, through a gap in a crumbling stone wall. It swings from a south to a westerly direction, following the line of another wall before crossing the footbridge over the river. The path then aims for Alport Castles Farm where a wide track heads down the valley. As it turns for Heyridge Farm, abandon it for a path descending into some woods to the Snake Road.

Across the road, follow a track that leads to a ford across the River Ashop. A nearby footbridge allows a drier crossing of the river. Rejoin the track and follow it eastwards, skirting the hill slopes beneath Upper Ashop Farm. The grooved track, part of a Roman road linking forts near Glossop and Bradwell, climbs steadily across the rough grassy slopes of Blackley Hey. Ignore the left fork descending to Rowlee Bridge, but continue the climb to a gate with a sign denoting that this is the edge of open country (GR158879).

Those who want to stay the night at Edale Youth Hostel should carry straight on turning right along the bridleway at the next crossroads. If not, stay this side of the gate and double back, right, on a worn track westwards on the grassy slopes of Crookstone Hill. A signpost by a tree in the middle of the moor points the way to a stile in the intake wall. From here the path wends its way through moors of heather and bilberry to the skyline crags on Crookstone Out Moor. From the crags a narrow path traces the edge. At the head of Lady Brook Clough would-be youth hostellers have a second chance to leave the high route. These may be the

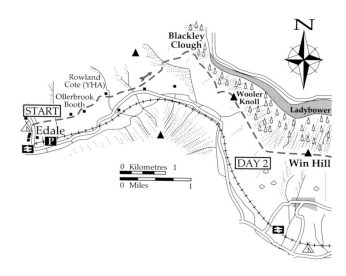

best moments of the day with superb views over Edale's pastures to the Mam Tor ridge, and most walkers will wish to prolong them by staying high. The path encounters a series of rock features – Ringing Roger, which has a bird's-eye view over Edale village; Nether Tor, a huge outcrop and Upper Tor.

All good things must come to an end, however, and this day ends with a descent along the former Pennine Way route down Grindsbrook Clough, which begins by a huge cairn. After an uneasy start through a bouldery ravine, a well-defined path takes the route down to Edale village.

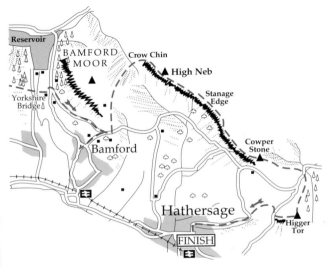

Day 2: 14 miles/22km (12½ miles/20km from the youth hostel)

Those who started the day at the youth hostel will have a head start today for the route passes by its front door. The route begins on a walled track by the information centre and crosses Grinds Brook on a little stone bridge, before heading eastwards across fields to the farming hamlet of Ollerbrook Booth. Through the farmyard a stony lane continues east towards Cotefield farm. Take the path passing to the south of the latter, passing through a couple of gates and a stile.

A sign, 'Footpath to open country' (easily missed), marks the spot where the path divides. The one to be followed leaves the track, climbing left by a hedge and above some woodland. The path, now at the foot of the moor, threads through gorse, bracken and hawthorn trees to the car park of Edale Youth Hostel. Pass immediately in front of the main building, pleasantly situated among mixed woodland, and descend some steps to cross a footbridge over Lady Brook Clough.

The path now climbs the opposite banks to contour round a bracken-cloaked moorland spur back into the main valley. It fords the stream in the partially-wooded Jaggers Clough, before climbing once more to high pastureland on a hillside that separates Edale from the Woodlands valleys. One of Ladybower Reservoir's fingers stretches out among dense conifers on the east side of the slopes.

On reaching the five-way junction of tracks at the ridge turn right along the Roman road to the medieval Hope Cross. Keep to the path on the left of the wall. This climbs along the ridge all the way to the summit of Win Hill, a rocky crest jutting out from a sea of heather. Win Hill has one of the Peak's best views – a 360 degree panorama across Edale, the Hope and Woodlands valleys to most of the hills. Scramble across the rocky crest and descend on a wide eroded eastbound path into Winhill Plantation, where a clear path descends in the shade of conifers to the lane just north of Yorkshire Bridge. Follow first the lane to the main road, then New Road, which is staggered to the left on the other side. It climbs beneath the rocks of Bamford Edge giving good views down the Derwent valley and the heather-clad rocky peak of Carl Wark.

A quarry track on the bend at GR216839 leads to the old excavations. Beyond these the marked path fades. Be content to head north to the shoulder of Bamford Moor, where Stanage Edge will be seen at its best, rising from a moorland col. Traverse the marshy col, aiming for the rocks of Crow Chin. A grassy gap allows the walker an easy route between the cliffs to the ridge top: a climber may choose an even more entertaining approach.

A good path follows the top edge of the gritstone cliffs south-east to the summit trig point on High Neb, where the heather moors decline towards the back yards of Sheffield. The easy but spectacular stroll continues over a second, but unnamed, summit to reach the road at Upper Burbage Bridge. Higger Tor is the next objective. There are two paths. The higher one is best, heading southwards across the heather along Fiddler's Elbow to the top of the shapely gritstone hill.

From the summit, follow the little path along the southern edge of the Tor. Eventually it winds back to the road at the 372 spot height (GR253818), where a walled track wiggles across the slopes of Callow to reach another road descending Dale Bottom into Hathersage.

Transport

Cars provide the visitor with a most convenient way into the Peak National Park, but they also provide the authorities with their biggest problems – congestion and pollution. Walkers may find that by making more use of public transport they can plan better routes without the encumbrance of a car. Often car parks are too far from the hill or involve some road-walking.

Trains: Regular trains run between Manchester Piccadilly and Sheffield stopping at New Mills, Edale, Hope, Bamford and Hathersage. Regular trains run between Blackpool North and Buxton via Bolton, Manchester Piccadilly and Oxford Road, Stockport, Chapel-en-le-Frith and Dove Holes.

Buses: The bus timetables throughout the Peak vary considerably on the time of the year and day of the week. On summer Sundays the services are quite comprehensive, but on winter weekdays this is not the case. Detailed information can be obtained from: The Public Transport Unit, Derbyshire County Council, Freepost, Chatsworth Hall, Matlock, Derbyshire, DE4 9BR or telephone 01629 580000 (ext. 6746). They supply complete bus/rail timetables for the Peak at £1.20 each including postage (1996 rates). The booklets are also available from Tourist Information Centres.

Useful addresses

Tourist Information Centres

Buxton: The Crescent, Derbyshire, SK17 6BQ. 01298 25106.

Glossop: Station Forecourt, Norfolk, St SK13 8BS. 01457 855920.

Macclesfield: Town Hall, Market Place, Cheshire, SK10 1HR. 01625 504112.

Leek: Market Place, Staffs, ST13 5HH. 01538 381000.

National Park Visitor Centres:

Castleton: 01433 620679. Open Easter to end of October and weekends.

Edale: 01433 620207.

Fairholmes (by Derwent Reservoir): 01433 650953. Open Easter to end of October and weekends.

Langsett Barn: 01226 370770. Open Easter to end of October and weekends.

Torside (Longdendale Valley): 01433 620207. Open Easter to end of October and weekends.

Peak National Park (Head Office): Aldern House, Baslow Road, Bakewell, Derbyshire, DE45 1BE. 01629 816200.

The Ramblers' Association:

1-5 Wandsworth Road, London, SW8 2XX. 0171 582 6878.

Public Transport Unit, Derbyshire County Council:

Freepost, Chatsworth Hall, Matlock, Derbyshire, DE4 9BR. 01629 580000 (ext 6746).

Index